Praise

"*Speaking Architecture* has allowed me to understand the realities of a true architectural practice. This concise yet extensive exposition navigates the evolution of design and brings transparency to a complex system, making this book an essential resource for anyone who intersects with our built environment. Jeff Klymson illuminates the process of transforming a concept into a space for life."
 — **Trevor Lord**, Business Development Director, Boldt Construction

"*Speaking Architecture* is a much-needed resource for anyone considering working with an architect or planning a construction project. This valuable, accessible book expertly guides the reader through the entire architect-client process, meticulously detailing each stage, and shares numerous insightful anecdotes and indispensable wisdom. *Speaking Architecture* empowers individuals to gain a thorough understanding of the design and construction process allowing them to actively contribute to its success."
 — **Carlo Parente**, Architect and Assistant Professor, Toronto Metropolitan University

"There is a clear and personal voice of experience in *Speaking Architecture*, one that resonates with years of listening to and observing clients and contractors, and engaging them into a conversation with the goal of ensuring a more fulfilling and creative building project."

— **Richard Nelson**, Architect

"*Speaking Architecture* is a resource of broad appeal and enduring value for everyone involved in bringing a building concept from imagination to reality. It will remain close at hand in my own practice in the years to come."

— **Lamar Johnson**, Founder and Executive Chairman, Lamar Johnson Collaborative

JEFF KLYMSON Architect

Speaking Architecture
From Concept to Construction to Completion

Re think

First published in Great Britain in 2023
by Rethink Press (www.rethinkpress.com)

© Copyright Jeff Klymson

All rights reserved. No part of this publication may be reproduced, stored in or introduced into a retrieval system, or transmitted, in any form, or by any means (electronic, mechanical, photocopying, recording or otherwise) without the prior written permission of the publisher.

The right of Jeff Klymson to be identified as the author of this work has been asserted by him in accordance with the Copyright, Designs and Patents Act 1988.

This book is sold subject to the condition that it shall not, by way of trade or otherwise, be lent, resold, hired out, or otherwise circulated without the publisher's prior consent in any form of binding or cover other than that in which it is published and without a similar condition including this condition being imposed on the subsequent purchaser.

Cover image © Jeff Klymson and Collective Office

This book is dedicated to Margaret, Sarah, and Elise, the three strongest people I know. I love you all, thank you for your kindness and support.

Further thanks to Lamar Johnson, Carlo Parente, Rick Nelson, Trevor Lord, and our Collective Office team – without your dedication this work would not be possible.

Contents

Foreword	1
Introduction	5
PART ONE Defining Your Project	**11**
1 The Big Idea	13
Writing a starting statement	14
Clarifying the scope of your project	17
Finding an architect	19
Developing a project definition with your architect	21
Establishing your project team	26
Letting your architect be an architect	31
Working with an architect you know	35
Practical thoughts on defining your project	37

2	**Scheduling and Budgeting**	**39**
	Creating your schedule	40
	Calculating your project budget	43
	Cost-plus, guaranteed maximum price, and change orders	48
	Understanding the terms 'pre-construction', 'value engineering' and 'pro forma'	50
	Thinking differently about cost	52
	Considering costs over your project's lifecycle	55
	Practical thoughts on scheduling and budgeting	57
3	**Communicating During The Project**	**59**
	Using email, text, and apps	60
	Making decisions	64
	Setting project goals	67
	Aligning your personal finances	71
	Practical thoughts on project communication	74
PART TWO	**Designing Your Project**	**75**
4	**Getting Started**	**77**
	Understanding the role of your architect	78
	Signing an agreement with your architect	82
	Understanding your architect's work	86

	Understanding contract documents	88
	Using 3D renderings	95
	Adding an interior designer to your project	96
	Handling furniture, fixtures and equipment (FFE)	97
	Practical thoughts on working with your architect	100
5	**Working With Your Engineers**	**103**
	Structural engineers	106
	Soil testing and geotechnical engineers	107
	Mechanical (HVAC) engineers	109
	Electrical engineers	112
	Plumbing engineers (water and sewer)	113
	Practical thoughts on engineers	115
PART THREE	**Building Your Project**	**117**
6	**Getting Permission To Build**	**119**
	Working with a permit expediter	123
	Your local Authority Having Jurisdiction (AHJ)	125
	Building codes and your permit	127
	The permit application process and costs	131
	Local permit strategies	133
	Practical thoughts on permit or permission to build	134

7	**Working With Your General Contractor**	**137**
	Design-bid-build	138
	Design-preconstruction-build	139
	Design-build	139
	Understanding the general contractor's role	141
	Signing a general contractor's agreement	146
	Working with subcontractors	148
	Starting the construction process	151
	Detailed schedule	151
	Contract administration	153
	Inspections and punch lists	156
	Practical thoughts on contractors	159
8	**Living In Your Project**	**161**
9	**Conclusion**	**165**
Glossary		**169**
Directory		**199**
Acknowledgments		**207**
The Author		**209**

Foreword

The fable of the blind men and the elephant tells of a group of blind men who seek to describe an elephant without being able to visualize and conceive of the total animal. Over more than 40 years in architecture across project types and geographies, working with clients both large and small, one of the supreme challenges faced in my practice is converting the vision of clients who can only see a small piece of the picture (usually only the finished project) into an integrated process that is understandable to all who must be involved. Now, my long-time colleague and collaborator Jeff Klymson has created a resource to tackle that problem and give all parties a common understanding of the total "elephant".

SPEAKING ARCHITECTURE

Speaking Architecture provides first-time property owners and investors a pathway to successful completion of a project that meets the needs of the user or owner for whom it is being built. Whether building a home, office building or warehouse, no contracts should be executed or dollars exchanged without a step-by-step design and development process and a thorough understanding of the roles of the architect, consultant and contractor. The experience and resources offered in *Speaking Architecture* allows prospective owners to be in control of the project and to avoid common pitfalls that can cause delays, cost overruns, and unmet expectations.

By framing the architectural process in language understandable to the novice, *Speaking Architecture* also serves as a critical resource for architects and contractors involved with clients who are not familiar with architecture projects. Through the use of "architect's anecdotes" drawn from his 20 years of experience in the field, Klymson gives architects a tool to use in communicating to clients throughout the project, increasing client satisfaction and enhancing relationships.

To the uninitiated, the architecture and construction process is filled with unfamiliar jargon, regulations, and interdependencies. Klymson has demystified this process by focusing on three key activities: 1) Defining the Project, 2) Designing the Project, and 3) Building the Project. He draws on his varied experience with

FOREWORD

a broad project set to simplify an otherwise complex process into clear, understandable terms and steps.

Speaking Architecture is a resource of broad appeal and enduring value for everyone involved in bringing a building concept from imagination to reality. It will remain close at hand in my own practice in the years to come.

Lamar Johnson
Founder and Executive Chairman
Lamar Johnson Collaborative, https://theljc.com

Introduction

If you've picked up this book, it is safe to assume you have a desire to know more about architecture. It might be a passing interest. You may simply have some time in an airport between flights, who knows, but it is most likely because you are considering a construction project of some kind. In this case, simply knowing that architects are the people who design buildings isn't enough. What does 'design' mean in the context of construction? Where does architecture meet structural engineering, for example? Who decides what materials to use? Who draws which plans? When? How do you move from design into construction? What should you ask potential general contractors? What does a structural engineer do? Who do you congratulate when things go well? Who do you look to if things go badly? All these questions, and many more, are covered in *Speaking Architecture.*

It is possible you are about to invest in a staggeringly ambitious institutional project in Dubai or Jiangsu, China. In which case, your flight is probably First Class. As I write, I am, however, imagining someone, somewhere, with more day-to-day dreams; a home or small business project, perhaps with a couple of floors; warm in winter, cool in summer and with lots of natural light. It's easy to assume this second case is somehow less important, of lower value and doesn't quite matter as much as the first. My response is that is nonsense. The key to this book is my firm belief that all buildings matter. Every building has an owner, and every owner has a vision of what they want the building to be like when it is finished. All architecture is the same. It is the practice of turning that owner's vision into reality and everyone has something to gain from understanding its practices and processes.

The problem is largely that the public perception of architects and architecture comes from a handful of famous examples. The type of architects that rise to prominence tend to lead significant projects from the front and their names appear on plaques, in the museums, galleries, government buildings and corporate headquarters they design. Players on the international stage, their names become synonymous with large egos and larger budgets and opinions on their work fill column inches across the world's media. It must be

INTRODUCTION

said, I am not one of those architects. I am, however, one of these hard-working professionals. I spend my days working calmly and collaboratively with little fanfare alongside other skilled professionals to make owner visions become real.

I was born in Vancouver, Canada, and raised in a smaller town forty miles east of there. I went to kindergarten in a one-room schoolhouse and elementary school just down the block from my house. I grew up on the edge of a forest, which was my backyard. I moved with my family to the city of Toronto at the age of nine, where we lived in a neighborhood much different from where I grew up. My father was a contractor and I worked for him in construction in the summers and on weekends from the age of fourteen to the end of my undergraduate education. I went to architectural school at Ryerson University in Toronto (now Toronto Metropolitan University), earning a Bachelor of Architectural Science. I then moved to Chicago in my mid-twenties to attend the Illinois Institute of Technology's College of Architecture. I graduated with a Master of Architecture degree from there and set to work.

I founded my own business, Collective Office, in 2009. Collective Office is an architecture practice which creates thoughtful spaces that help people live more purposeful, peaceful, and productive lives. We have since collectively designed more than 300 projects and seen 215 of them built. This totals approximately

$98 million in construction value. In that time, we have had many amazing successes and a few awards. We have had projects that have run perfectly to schedule where we handed the keys to the client on the prescribed day with much fanfare. There may have been a ribbon to cut, and we made sure to capture photos of happy clients to share with the world. We have also had a few projects where that didn't happen. The keys were handed over accompanied by an apology and stressful contractual wrangling. The good news: we learned from both cases. What is more, the lessons are in your hands right now.

This book is primarily for prospective architecture clients. If you're planning a construction project, being forewarned is forearmed. I'll share steps you can take to avoid common pitfalls and reduce the risk of cost overruns and schedule delays. I will also cut through our profession's jargon and share more than a couple of trade secrets. Overall, the main lesson is that projects with a strong foundation, team, and direction are more likely to enjoy success when everyone involved speaks a common language – the language of architecture.

This book is intended to be a primer and introduction that makes any architectural processes you find opaque clearer and more transparent. It has been written to provide resources you can directly use during a project and act as a roadmap to understanding the basics of architecture at each phase of design and

INTRODUCTION

construction activity. I hope you'll reach for it throughout the course of your project. If you're in the middle of a project and you sense things are stalling or veering off-path, there'll be lessons to help get you back on track here. Whether you're operating as a private individual and investing in a new home, for example, or leading a commercial project for your employer, you will be able to apply lessons to your tasks immediately. In the spirit of sharing knowledge, I think other architects, contractors, financial stakeholders, educators, and students may also find value in this book.

I have structured the content that follows into three sections: defining your project, designing your project, and building your project. Each of these sections converge and overlap. I've also included a short epilogue to give you tips about living in your project once the process is complete. I have written directly and unashamedly from my own experience. I have included various anecdotes to support my arguments and conclusions throughout the text. All these anecdotes are based on real case studies and genuine projects. I have changed some of the details to spare people's blushes (often my own), but rest assured, the spirit of each story is true and the learning point, I trust, will be clear. I have also included practical thoughts at the end of each chapter. These are key takeaways in bullet-point form that I trust will be easy to remember.

After you've read the book, I would like to think you will have an air of confidence around you as you navigate your construction project. My gift to you is a firmer grasp of how architects and their collaborators work and how to communicate with them.

Whatever construction style or scope of the construction project you are embarking on, I would encourage you to take *Speaking Architecture* along with you on your project. Think of it in the same way that you might think of a travel guide to a far-flung destination or a phrase book in a language you haven't quite mastered yet. Read it from cover to cover by all means, but also dip in and out as the need, or mood, takes you. It has been designed as a practical rather than theoretical guide. Wherever it takes you, I wish you well.

PART ONE
DEFINING YOUR PROJECT

1
The Big Idea

So, you've decided to build something. The opening part of this book assumes that's as far as you have gone in your journey. Have you decided on a dream house to retire in? Do you want to extend your home for your growing family? Do you need a home office? Do you want to add value to a property? Do you want to make a positive difference in a community? It doesn't matter why you're starting a project. The process is the same. It starts by figuring out exactly what it is that you want to do. Once you know that, you can find the team that will make it happen.

It sounds daunting, but it shouldn't be. I'll show you how to go about it.

Writing a starting statement

Human history is a sequence of amazing moments. This includes new building projects. Given that designing projects is complex, the realization that all buildings start with a new and unique moment of inspiration is especially important. It is easy to make assumptions and fall back on previous experiences. Forgetting that all architecture projects start from a fresh, new individual vision can cause costly mistakes, and amazing new ideas can be overlooked.

Everyone involved in the design and construction of a building needs to understand the big idea behind it. What is the end goal? What is the project aiming to achieve? The initial idea needs capturing somehow. The tool architects use to do this is often referred to as a concept, or starting statement. This ought to be a short, definitive statement that records a moment in time and grounds the project in tangible language.

The value of being able to start a project by succinctly capturing and sharing the reasons a project exists cannot be stressed enough. It is important for many reasons. The first is that we are human – exceptional, but limited in our own ways. Construction projects are complex with a lot of moving parts with long timelines that require long-term focus from multiple participants. Human nature means we easily get distracted. Group thinking can, and often does, meander off course without discipline. A starting statement grounds the project firmly and gives the architect, the design team, and anyone related to the project, something to refer to. It reminds everyone working on a project why the project exists, so they can realign their work at any point, if required. Every project is constantly pulled off course. It's the nature of working with collaborators over time to create something new, no matter how simple.

Society's modern methods of working do not help. We are ever more connected in today's transactional world and stimulated to a point of saturation. We can get dozens of emails, with differing opinions, before 10am. We can build 3D models that present alternative visions, prompt questions, and open up opportunities for change. We have, it seems, endless choices. At the end of the day, however, success comes from handling all the inputs and pressures that come our way during the design and construction of a project. A clear and concise Concept or Starting Statement gives everyone a shared reference point. This allows regular check-ins. Are we still all heading toward the same goal? Are we still on course? It is easier to get back on track during stressful periods by referring back to a Concept or Starting Statement. There will always be stressful periods. They are part and parcel of every construction project.

ARCHITECT'S ANECDOTE:
The value of a starting statement

A robust starting statement is useful to establish architect and client alignments. Imagine upgrading a historic home, for example. There is often an inherent conflict between new and original features. I worked with a client who had fallen in love with their new home's existing features, brick facade, original doors, cornices, interior fireplace, and so on. But they also wanted new features and, specifically, wanted to raise their second-floor ceilings from 8ft to 12ft. This was fine, except for the plan to reuse the original doors. These original 7ft doors reinstalled with 12ft ceilings meant a compromise had to be struck.

During the initial conversation with the client, we hadn't assumed anything. Nor had we referred to similar projects or previous iterations of plans or designs. We came at it anew. This meant drafting a starting statement that described the project as delivering a modernized, airy, light, and spacious project. Through reminding the client of their original primary desire, and having helpfully expressed it in writing, the 12ft ceilings won out and the 7ft doors were designed into another role in the project elsewhere.

When distractions present themselves, it is important to be flexible, informed, and organized to find the best path forward. In the door scenario above, we worked hard to find the best solution for the client's wish, but, ultimately, needed to return to the starting statement to realign the project and our clients to the overall goal. Doing so took enough of the emotion out of the decision-making process to proceed to the right solution.

Clarifying the scope of your project

Let us assume you've written a starting statement or concept you are happy with. It is exciting and marks a major milestone. There is not, however, enough detail in this short concept statement to fully define your project. This is where you need a scope document, but what does it mean to define the scope of your project? This answer is both complicated and straightforward. On one hand, the scope document is a wish list that tells your architect, and everyone else who is interested, the features you want in your project. The document forms a list that becomes the basis for your architect to create your project which can be used for budgeting purposes. This document also becomes the basis for understanding the investment required to make your vision a reality. The scope document will also allow a basic schedule or timeline to be created. What deadlines are realistic? When does work need to start?

The scope document becomes complicated when you start to organize the information within it. Do you do it room by room, or element by element? You could also list by priority: must-haves and nice-to-haves, for example. What is essential? What can you add if budget and time allow?

You might not have done enough detailed planning to know about some aspects of your list at this early stage. Plumbing and electrical systems, foundations and structural elements might require further information to understand their role and potential costs. However, the scope document can be a live document that evolves with the project and becomes more detailed as information is available. Define the scope document well, and you can save yourself a lot of time, effort, and money. Do it badly, and you will be surprised by the unexpected costs as the project develops.

ARCHITECT'S ANECDOTE:
The value of a good scope document

All ideas require interpretation and then translation to execute. One of our clients wanted to update their bathroom vanities and saw an image online of a furniture cabinet with a sink and wall faucet and a hanging light fixture. The mirror was also a medicine cabinet for storage. This image finished off the client's dream bathroom. They wanted this and were committed to having it in their home.

After a quick meeting, a bathroom fixture vendor responded that it was easy and they began to order the fixtures. They didn't, however, have a conversation with me about finding the piece of furniture, its size, its installation requirements, how the water supply and drain plumbed in, whether the sink was integrated into the cabinet, or how the faucet was attached to the wall. We hadn't written an adequate project scope document, so the drawings that would describe this still needed to be created.

I call this the 'project decision effect'. A small request, decision, or change may seem straightforward on the surface, but has a wide reach beyond first impressions. In a project with a vague, poorly thought-through scope (like this bathroom vanity), the simplest of choices will have a major impact on schedules and costs. Success starts by drafting a project scope document that is thorough and detailed.

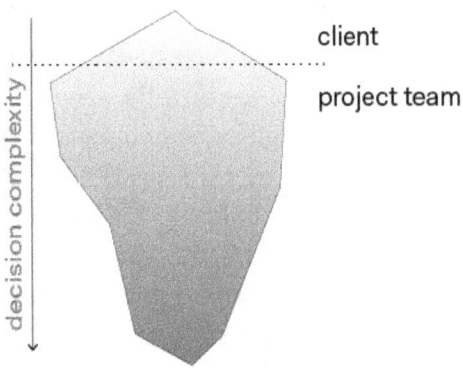

The 'project decision effect'

Finding an architect

Clients can find architects in any number of ways, but the process should always be handled with a great deal of care. It ought to feel like a genuine meeting of minds and it is vital to feel you are in a productive partnership from the beginning of any project.

A great place to start looking for an architect beyond family and friends, if you're in the US, is your local American Institute of Architects (AIA). These chapters have member firms lists with awards and commendations for successful projects. Past award submissions and winners are available for anyone in the market for help to see. In most cases, it will be easy to seek and find projects in alignment with your own goals and style. Find three to five companies that are appropriate and contact them to set up an initial call. If that goes well, then make an appointment to visit their office and see how they work. An in-person feel for whether their personalities and office culture fit with your way of working is as important as an architect's technical ability. In the case of the latter, ask to see portfolio projects that are similar to what you are trying to achieve, and don't be afraid to ask questions about design, process, lessons learned, and past project costs, including the architect's fees and construction costs. Finally, make sure to ask for references that you can follow up on and then pick up the phone and do it.

Once you've made a choice, the best onboarding processes employ a series of conversations designed to make sure both parties understand the project, each other, and the proposed steps forward. Some architects use simple questionnaires to formalize the process. Clients, on their part, should undertake thorough reviews of an architect's current and past work. Reputable architects should be open and transparent to make this easy. The task for both parties is to discover alignments, establish a common language, and to create trust. The team's personalities have an important role to play. A good 'fit' is often hard to define, but you know when it happens.

There is a danger in approaching a project with preconceptions on either side. The relationship between architect and client ought to be based on an initial transformative evaluation and testing ideas. It is an opportunity to look at a project with fresh new eyes. This works best if the client arrives with an open mind and the architect commits to finding the right path to success.

Developing a project definition with your architect

If you've followed steps one to three above, you will now have a starting statement that encapsulates the concept, your project goals, and a project scope document that proposes a route to get there. You will also have started talking to an architect you feel a genuine connection with. As a client, it's tempting to think the work is done. At this stage, however, it is just beginning.

All design projects are unique creative endeavors. They rarely move from start to finish in a linear fashion. They evolve during their timeline and successfully maintaining a schedule, controlling costs, and limiting unforeseen circumstances is achieved by managing this evolution carefully. This means

SPEAKING ARCHITECTURE

developing a fuller project scope document in partnership with your architect to ensure you are both heading in the same direction.

This ought to take the form of a written description, or narrative, that breaks the project down into logical pieces. It can help to use the concept of scale to organize this effort. To ensure you get everything covered, start with the largest elements, create groups, and then define smaller and smaller elements within those groups. It is important that you and your architect agree on a shared view of how to proceed. Misalignment, once the project is underway, can be frustrating and costly to address.

This definition process ought to focus on how the project will look, and then how it should feel. As a written narrative develops, you can begin to add visual examples to act as inspiration and provide illustrations for the narrative. Similarly, any examples of design drawings of features that produce the same qualities you desire in the project can be added. Without curation and commentary, however, it can be easy to misinterpret the intent of an image or diagram, so it is helpful to annotate these reference images with explanations that explain why they are relevant to the current project, and why they resonate. With only a small amount of direction, images and drawings can be essential communication tools whenever you are speaking the language of architecture.

THE BIG IDEA

Together, the written narrative and visual examples should evolve your project scope document. The more detailed your scope document the better, this document will be referred to repeatedly during the project. It should focus on conversations and meetings and decision-making across the project team. Inspired by the way filmmakers plot and plan their work, the term 'storyboard' could be used to describe this document. It should be considered a live document that can evolve and be updated as the project progresses, but it's also the document on which the contract between your architect and contractor will be based.

Although primarily for the project team, there is a wider audience for the project drawings and documents. As well as the client and architect, consultants to the architect, planning authorities, and potential contractors may need to review your project plans. In the US, the Authority Having Jurisdiction (known as the AHJ) will need to review and approve your drawings and documents in order to receive a building permit, and perform inspections.

Many people will have varying degrees of involvement in the project. However, there is one common thread: the drawings and documents that are created by the architect and their team as part of the project process. Most modern drawing and document packages are typically accompanied by 3D visualizations that convey the complete idea in order to facilitate understanding and approval of the project prior to starting work. Appropriate parts of the 'storyboard' can be included in presentations too, along with actual design features to better describe the projected intent. After all, the drawings and documents that are created for a project are a format that is historically accepted by which information is exchanged in order to understand how the project will happen.

Drawings are created from scratch each time a new project is undertaken. Architects work with many 'conventional' drawing types (plans, sections, elevations, etc) and documents. Outputs are always unique to each project. Many of these will be flat, two-dimensional drawings solving three-dimensional conditions. As a client, it is worth putting in the time to understand how these are understood, interpreted, and translated. Some scenarios may need more exploration and require more conversations to ensure everyone is on the same page.

A well-defined and documented project is essential before work continues. Finding a balance between an architect's technical work and the client's vision is important. The objective is to ensure everything that follows is a collective collaboration towards an agreed outcome.

We use design as a tool in an iterative manner to solve each situation until it satisfies the project for the individual client. We keep designing until the project is

THE BIG IDEA

resolved or it needs to be built, which is often a function of the time we are given for our process. We keep designing even when the project is in construction, trying to make every element better. For the architect, design never stops.

ARCHITECT'S ANECDOTE:
A changing scope

We began working with a new client on their vacation house. They had acquired three lots for the project. One would become the driveway access to the main road and the other two would be built on. The client was looking for an efficient and minimal four-bedroom house. They also wanted a separate garage, pool, and a future guest house. We began our process by designing a basic series of house space plans responding to the client's needs, the site, and neighbors. The initial task was to locate the house, pool, garage, and guest house on these two lots; it was very tight but we worked hard to find a solution. We started with the focus on the house while confirming that a reasonably sized pool, garage, and future guest house could work on this site.

We were wrapping up the initial design phases for the house when we received an email from the client saying they had acquired two more lots. We got our hands on the updated survey and immediately saw much more opportunity with the arrangement of the buildings on the site.

The client had never mentioned that they were even interested in, or considering purchasing more land for the project. They thought we would just move the house as it had been designed to date over to the center of the new overall site and let the other elements follow. However, changing a site always presents new opportunities because the site is key for the design of every project. Some of the most important elements to consider on a site are light, views, access, and privacy. Good architecture provides an outdoor connection to indoor space too. The project needs to respond to all these as well as the client's needs and wants.

When the buildable site doubled, the project immediately presented so much new opportunity. It resolved the issues that we were facing with too many elements on a small site, but the initial definition would have been more successful and a smoother process if we'd known that the client was trying to obtain more land from the beginning. Changing scope is never as efficient as having all the information at a project's starting point.

Establishing your project team

A construction project team can be viewed in many ways, but perhaps the most useful is a series of layers, or strata. The project exists because it has been instigated by a client who wants to achieve or build something. The client is at the top of the project and this can be both exciting and daunting, but too daunting for some. If this is the case for you, there are mechanisms to assist. You can appoint someone, a friend or family member perhaps, to act on your behalf. There are also professionals that can be hired to act as client representatives or agents. These are often used if an individual client does not have the time or inclination to work through their project effectively themselves. Even if you are happy to take on the role and don't want formal representation, it is useful to have allies in your corner to provide feedback, help as a confident voice in the process, attend meetings for confirmation of direction, and simply check and validate your decisions.

Assuming that the client, or their representative, is the top layer of the project, we might illustrate a project team like this:

Every project begins in its own way, and it is challenging to be too prescriptive when it comes to recruiting your team. There are, however, a few tips I can share to shorten the process, along with some pitfalls to be aware of. It is a universal truth that projects have a lot of personalities, and everything runs more smoothly when they all get along.

Start by asking your closest circle of contacts – whether that means friends and family or people from your professional network – a few questions. Has anyone you trust undertaken a similar project? Have they met good contractors? Have they been impressed with the quality of a particular construction company's work? Your first task is to vet potential team members against your requirements. Can they do the job? Alignment of personalities are important too. Will working with them be a positive experience?

Architect	AHJ	General contractor
structural engineer mechanical engineer electrical engineer plumbing engineer surveyor civil engineer soil engineer geotechnical engineer shoring engineer landscape architect interior designer acoustic engineer lighting designer …	plans reviewers • structural • mechanical • electrical • plumbing • fire protection • accessibility … inspectors fire marshall historic preserv. environ. quality …	excavator concrete contractor framer mechanical contractor electrical contractor plumbing contractor millworker cabinet maker tile installer glass installer low voltage contractor trim carpenter …

Comprehensive project team

The main reason for suggesting checking with close contacts is the inherent level of mutual support such relationships present. Friends and family are likely to be frank and transparent when describing their experiences and so, you would hope, you will be able to trust the people they are recommending. It is important to feel you are getting an accurate description of a contractor's abilities and those recommending have clearly and accurately articulated their past experiences. We have discussed finding an architect earlier in the chapter, but this provides a useful reminder for them too.

At this stage, the most important team member to recruit next is the general contractor (often shortened to the abbreviation GC). Taking responsibility for realizing the design and building your project is a very different role to the architect and requires a very different skill set. Your architect is your primary advocate through the project design process, but it is logical to extend the project team to the contractor for the next stages of activity: pricing and undertaking the work itself. Phases can overlap and, indeed, will influence each other, but the traditional method is to separate the initial design process from bidding or pricing exercises. This allows the architect to create the best project design and suggest the best materials, finishes, and fixtures possible given the site, schedule, and investment without compromise.

It is vital, however, to hire a general contractor who understands the value of the architect's vision and is motivated to complete the project in line with it. The architect and general contractor relationship is a balancing act. It will be push-and-pull throughout the duration of your project. The general contractor must be willing to make compromises. They will often ask to change the project's design features and materials leading to a different outcome. Your architect will continue to use design to solve challenges that occur during planning and construction. These typically center around lowering costs while not sacrificing the design, experience, or materials.

The good news is when you have an architect and a general contractor that communicate well and work together to achieve the best project possible in a frictionless process, you have the right team. However, all these projects take on their own direction, and like all relationships, maintaining a positive architect and general contractor partnership takes a lot of ongoing work and effort. When more care is given to genuinely looking after each other's interests from the onset of projects, the result is a smooth, exciting, and rewarding process.

How do you choose your general contractor? If your architect has completed similar projects recently, it makes sense to explore existing relationships. Interviewing general contractors who already know your architect well is a handy shortcut. As well as checking for capability and 'fit', it is important to make sure that any general contractor you consider has the capacity and availability in their schedule for your project. There is little point in spending time chatting to a contractor who can't achieve your project deadlines, even if they wanted to.

Any selected general contractor will form a team of their own to complete the job. They will use subcontracted tradespeople such as framers, drywallers, electricians, plumbers, painters, etc. Confirming that subcontractors (often shortened to subs) are in place is a useful test that everything has been thought through for your project. Contractors that only have one 'sub' on their books for any discipline can be a risk. If they only know one electrician, for example, they are unlikely to get competitive pricing for the work, which will add to project costs. And that's before considering the risk of a single tradesperson being unavailable to work to your schedule.

Finding your project team does not need to be a difficult task. It is important to start with the architect and then the general contractor. Any other consultant, engineer, or tradesperson you need should stem from these two key players. It is important you spend enough time with both of them to feel comfortable with how they fit together. You will spend a considerable amount of time and energy with them for the duration of your project, so it's important that all your personalities work well together.

Projects operate on trust. Make sure that your architect and general contractor have demonstrated their capabilities through successful projects that feel similar to yours. If possible, try to visit any reference buildings and speak to the owners. Vet your team, request references, and follow up with them by asking pertinent in-depth questions. If that sounds combative, it is not meant to be. There's no need to be overly challenging or aggressive. In fact, it is important to spend quality time building connections within the team, especially early on. Have a meal or a coffee and speak about topics beyond your project. A human touch will make a valuable contribution to the project.

Letting your architect be an architect

Some architects have, perhaps unfairly, gained a reputation for being difficult to work with. They are often blamed when projects hit bumps in the road and criticized for being unable to make clients' wishes come true. Some of this is justified, I'm sure. Nobody is perfect. However, some of this stems from a misunderstanding of how architects go about their work and there are helpful steps that you, as the client, can take to avoid problems.

Every architect and architecture firm will have their own approach to the design process and use a design vocabulary that is philosophically meaningful to them, and which they are passionate about. They may use terms such as modernism, minimalism, contemporary, transitional, traditional, or classical, for example. They may also lean towards a local vernacular or style that exists where you live. If you're not clear, it is important that you ask for clarification and examples. In my experience, architects love explaining the architecture they love, so this should not be challenging for them. This is important because your project should have a connection with your chosen architect's interests. Architects can do anything; however, you will get the best results when your objectives sit within your designer's portfolio. Misalignment happens more frequently than we all might acknowledge and, at best, causes friction between you and your architect or your architect and the project. At worst, it can cause significant project delays and overspending.

Architects are professionals with substantial academic training and even more professional experience. Qualification requires a series of challenging professional licensure exams. The quickest path to becoming

THE BIG IDEA

a licensed (and insured) architect with enough experience to handle projects independently, and in practice, is about twelve to sixteen years. Many of the professionals you will come across will have considerably more experience than that, of course. They are likely to have designed a project that is similar, if not identical, to your own. In their minds, they have already begun imagining possibilities and resolved central ideas on the project before even putting pen to paper, which naturally puts them several steps ahead of you, as the client. You need to make sure you and your architect are meeting at the same place conceptually. To make the design process as efficient and informative as possible, you should not be afraid to slow the architect down and ensure they have understood and thoroughly considered your wishes. In turn, it is important that you remain open to the myriad of possibilities your architect may present.

Architects are often asked very early in a project process about their fees and work schedules. How much the design process will cost and how long it will take are, on the face of it, absolutely fair questions. Architects will typically respond with a fixed fee or hourly fee based on a percentage of the construction cost, but any calculations are based on the assumption the client, as the principal lead of the project, will make prompt and timely decisions. The architect, as well as the general contractor in the later stages of the project, will be constantly looking to the client to support the process by being ahead of the decision-making process

SPEAKING ARCHITECTURE

to keep the project on track. Your design professionals and contractors should keep enough information in front of you to keep ahead of the schedule, but it's up to you to recognize that these decisions are required. The project will slow or stop if they are not made. Fees and costs might increase too.

Today, clients are rarely expected to fully understand architectural drawings, but it can help if you gain an understanding of the basics: floor plans, elevations, etc. 3D renderings are common today, but they can lead to distraction and confusion. If you are asked to review 3D spatial features, for example, it may be unnecessary to consider materials, finishes, and colors even if you are looking at photo-realistic visualizations. Such visualizations are inherently subjective. The lighting, finishes, furniture, upholstery, and even the people and other entourage can often be presented by architects, but they are not always appropriate to discuss. To avoid misunderstanding and miscommunication, it is always worth asking why, as the client, you are being shown a drawing or diagram, so you know what to provide feedback on. Depending on the stage of the design, telling an architect that you dislike certain pieces of trim is less relevant than confirming you are happy with room spatial feel, for example.

The best way to manage the relationship with your architect is to picture yourself using the project in the future. Apply 'your life' as a layer in your mind's eye on top of any visualizations, drawings, and diagrams your architect presents to you. Does it feel right? It's an interesting thought experiment that will, perhaps, help you avoid getting snagged on details. The fact that technology has speeded everything up doesn't necessarily help us here. As the client, it is worth fighting the temptation to continually 'push the button' as you might with social media and to avoid feeling overstimulated. In the days of hand drawing, blue-and-white blueprints, and watercolor sketches, the process was slower and more meditative. After all, you have hired an architect because you felt aligned with them. Your goal should be working with deep mutual respect and joint understanding.

Working with an architect you know

Chances are you already know an architect socially, or you may know someone that knows an architect, or maybe someone in your family is an architect. It seems natural to involve someone close to you, or who knows you. It should be easier for them to design your project, and they may give you a break on the fee... Architects are often asked about their services for 'a friend' or a family member. Sometimes this is unavoidable for an architect or designer. A project starts with a few questions at a social event and before the architect can object, they've been hired. Sometimes, depending on the state of the architect's business, or the economy, it can be hard for them to turn projects down.

Working with friends and family is not normally recommended, as it can be more emotionally trying than a standard business relationship. Motivations may be misaligned and there are inherent stresses that come with the baggage of existing personal relationships. This isn't unusual. The well-established paradigm around keeping a healthy distance between a client and a professional is mirrored in many other fields. Think of doctors and financial advisers. When you add a pre-existing friendship into the mix, it changes the energy between parties. The client-professional relationship works best when matters are black-and-white and purely professional in nature.

If their role is clearly defined, boundaries are established, and maybe even some level of compensation agreed, it can be helpful to have a friend who is an architect or design professional on your side. The reason is quite simple: the ability to translate the language of architecture for you. Architecture, design, and construction are complex and nuanced. They have a language of their own. Having an advocate that speaks this language and can help translate points into everyday language can prove to be valuable. This may be as simple as looking over the project starting point, scope, and definition documents or checking the contract (although this shouldn't be confused with legal guidance). It could be more involved and include a role for the duration of the project, or simply acting as a sounding board. The point here is that you needn't work alone. There is an abundance of design resources available for clients at all levels of need. Never be afraid to ask for help. Finding the appropriate resources is important and could be the difference between success and failure.

Practical thoughts on defining your project

1. Use a written narrative, precedent projects, and images to develop your project starting point. You need to agree with your architect on how you will provide input during the definition phases of the project. Once you have this 'homework', finish it as soon as possible. Your architect will need to understand your mindset and ambition before really digging into your project.

2. Engage with defining your project. Ask your architect how they will approach the design process and see if they can create a visual roadmap or storyboard. This can help you understand the actual amount of architectural scope that is required for your project. It may also help organize the entire project early on for all involved and can also be used as a reference for the duration of the project to describe your position.

3. Decide on your role. If you don't want to have a leadership role in the design process, make that clear and discuss alternative arrangements with your architect in the early phases of the project. Architects are professionals with a lot of education

and practical experience, which means they can be flexible, manage many work streams, and operate quickly. When the role of the client isn't clear, this slows the process down. Architects like the analogy of staying in one's lane. If everyone does the same, projects run more smoothly.

2
Scheduling and Budgeting

Once you have your architect and general contractor in place, you can take the work you've done in your project definition phase to begin to calculate the level of investment required to complete the project (budget) and the amount of time this will take (schedule). A good architect continually mediates these factors against project quality. Keep in mind that your architect will need to design the project before your contractor can obtain current real numbers from their subcontractors.

Construction is a long-lasting investment that succeeds when the building quality matches the design intent, and because architecture makes a lasting mark on our world, this could be judged over decades, or even centuries. Balancing financial investment, time, and quality therefore becomes complex. Schedule and budget will have relative value ranges given the place, time, and type of your project. The project definition process will determine what points in this value range are appropriate for your circumstances. As a general rule, however, it is the lasting architecture and experience that endure over time, so building quality is perhaps the best overall benchmark for success.

Creating your schedule

Is time and schedule important to you? Many would assume that a project simply needs to be delivered as quickly as possible, but that is forgetting everyone has a unique lifestyle and set of experiences and pressures. Time pressure is personal; the definition of 'as soon as possible' is unique to an individual's situation. People can be so pressured to complete a project that it's more important to them than the cost of the project or its quality. Conversely, others are not pressured by time at all. It is not uncommon for construction times to stretch – some even double or triple in length. Project schedules can also be dictated by formalities from AHJs, inspectors, or suppliers. These parties can add considerable time because of their pressures – often without any recourse. Depending on your location, some AHJs may issue building permits, for example, in weeks, maybe even days, while some may take a year or more. All this will need to be considered in an

SCHEDULING AND BUDGETING

early discussion with your architect to understand the time required for these aspects.

The best strategy is to include a schedule in your project definition phase of activity that takes into account all the pressures, priorities, and circumstances surrounding your project. The schedule expectation should be made clear to everyone from the client through to the architect and general contractor, to the entire project team. It is important the schedule is viewed as a living document that can be revised and iterated during the project.

Architects play a key role in managing project schedules. As things change, we continually switch between trying to stick to a specific timeline for a process, or changing it for the greater good. It's a balancing act that needs pragmatic, logical, calm, and collected decision-making. This is because a good architect and general contractor recognize that the schedule can quickly spiral out of control. Keeping a firm hand on it is perhaps the most important of all our skills.

At its core, a project schedule describes a sequence of events, from the initial stages through the design, approvals, and construction phases. While this is sequential in nature, it is more accurate to think in terms of layers, with overlaps for elements that can happen at the same time, or begin off site while another piece is happening in preparation. Parallel onsite and offsite tasks can meet to start a new stage.

This layered view of a timeline is more efficient than having each piece of scope start and finish before the next piece starts and finishes, like a single-track relay race. The diagram below illustrates the considerable time savings gained by adopting a layered rather than a simple linear path.

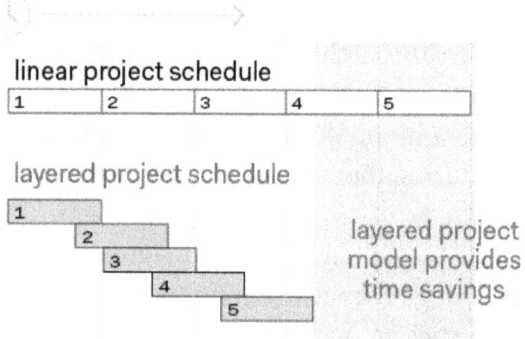

Linear vs layered approach

The point here is communicating your schedule and the pressures surrounding it is essential. Firstly, you need to agree on how important the schedule is compared to the budget and build quality. You may only have site access for a certain amount of time. You may have a fixed opening date for a public or commercial building. In these cases, your schedule may be priority. It is then important to communicate this to the project team and make sure the architect and general contractor know your deadlines. You could possibly write the importance of the schedule into your agreements with specific incentives or penalties to reinforce deadlines.

SCHEDULING AND BUDGETING

Calculating your project budget

Costs can vary considerably based on numerous factors, including location, time of the year, and environmental factors. Your budget has a relationship to the market, the labor force, material availability, and lending interest rates. Costs on your project can be determined at various stages and with different degrees of accuracy. Early in the project, you might get a broad ballpark figure which will normally be calculated with many caveats. Once the project is well defined, your general contractor should be able to obtain much more accurate pricing. It will, however, still come with caveats and contingencies to consider. For example, with an experienced team, the general contractor or architect may be able to look at recent similar projects and provide a range of costs per square foot for the project. If you have communicated your expectation of the finished project clearly, this could be used as a loose estimate for budgeting purposes. A general per-square-foot analysis of this kind can be very helpful upfront in your project to set expectations. Are you talking about a $500,000 or a $5,000,000 project? There is, however, a long process to work through the various design phases required to determine the actual project budget.

Any introduction to the finances of your project should begin with an understanding of the difference between hard and soft costs. Hard costs are direct construction costs for the project. This covers all the general contractor and subcontractor work. Hard costs are the materials and labor. Soft costs are the rest: architect's fees, other design professional costs, real estate, finance costs, permit costs, printing, travel, and so on. The general contractor's profit, overhead, and management fees are also considered soft costs. It is important to understand the difference between hard and soft costs when setting up the project structure. It's possible your lender will want to get involved too.

The financial structuring begins with the planning and design portions of the project. This often happens many months prior to construction starting. Conversations regarding finance strategies should happen during the initial consultation meetings with potential architects. Your lender may require a building permit, a formal project cost estimate, and a signed contract with your general contractor to allow a loan to close and begin drawing on it. This means pre-construction soft costs will need to be funded from elsewhere. The architect will, naturally, need to cover their overhead and costs so will typically want to invoice monthly. Reaching a satisfactory agreement to keep all sides happy allows the process to move seamlessly in its early phases.

Architects will also need to understand the plans to finance the project as a whole. Your architect and general contractor should be on the same page as you are throughout. Clear and transparent communication is important. Nothing stalls a project quite like running

SCHEDULING AND BUDGETING

out of money. Potential problems can come from your lender and may require building permit in hand, formal project cost estimate, signed contracts, or other pieces of paperwork to release the loan.

Once there is general agreement as to an estimated cost, the general contractor will send the project details out to their subcontractors and begin compiling all the numbers into a formal bid. This is a detailed breakdown of costs for you to approve. It is prudent here to discuss ancillary costs. One of the main ancillary costs is a contingency figure which covers reserve project funds that can be used if the predicted costs prove to be an underestimation. This amount of money is held in the central budget and can be used in the event of an unforeseen circumstance or change. An architectural project is a daunting task: it involves design, construction, many moving parts, lots of different parties, phases and stages, and decisions. Cost overruns are part of the course. The amount of contingency to include varies from project to project and, to a degree, depends on your attitude to risk.

For renovation projects, for example, architects typically recommend holding a contingency of 3–5% of your overall budget. If you encounter something unexpected, as is often the case with older buildings, additional costs can come from the contingency without having to go back to the lender for additional funds. Holding a contingency is an intelligent method of being careful and prepared for all projects.

All architectural projects take a great deal of time and effort and often change along the way. Your contingency can act as a lifeline and keep added stress and anxiety down. If it is not used, then it can be removed from the final loan amount at the end of construction. Think of this as an insurance line item in the project giving you peace of mind.

Lenders have many products that make completing projects attainable and more attractive. One of the best examples of this is a specific construction loan. Here, you receive funding in draws to perform the project, and then refinance back into a conventional mortgage, while keeping your hard-earned savings and investments working in the background passively.

If you're lucky enough to have savings or investments sufficient to fund your project, that remains an option too. It may be that you use capital to finance the early soft costs associated with the initial phases of the project. Architects will often treat projects that are designed for real estate transactions differently than those for owner occupancy. These projects can put pressures on design that work in opposition to the goals and objectives that make the best possible experience.

Discussing costs can be daunting, especially in the North American market. The terms budget, pricing, and costing are somewhat interchangeable. It is, however, very important for everyone to be on the same page when it comes to budget throughout.

The term 'budget' is often misused, which can lead to misunderstanding, particularly at the early stages of a project. People often use this term to apply to a maximum figure they are able to spend, but without any correlation to their wish list or project goals, this means very little. The term 'budget' should be used after the project scope is adequately defined, designed by your architect, and priced by your general contractor. For a budget to be adequately established, there must be an alignment of the money you have available to spend and a defined realistic project scope of work. Disconnects occur when the scope is too large for the amount of money available or vice versa.

While 'cost' is often used to describe the value of goods and materials and 'price' refers to a combination of materials and labor, realistically, the two words are synonymous. Your architect and general contractor should be able to collate costs and prices for all the pieces of the scope necessary for the project. To do this, the project needs to be defined in enough detail for a range of suppliers and subcontractors to understand.

This budgeting exercise can be exciting, but having a loosely defined scope or poorly resolved project can lead to a phenomenon referred to as scope creep. This occurs when everyone looking at pricing the project lacks the understanding necessary to be accurate and substitutions and extra items, and costs, find their way onto the project goals and objectives. Scope creep can also occur when multiple conversations are happening with the project stakeholders, and additions are made after the initial project was designed and priced. It is something to guard against as the budget takes shape.

Cost-plus, guaranteed maximum price, and change orders

Once a budget is agreed upon and the project gets a green light, there are different contract models to consider. It is common for residential project general contractors to use a cost-plus or time and materials agreement with the homeowners. These agreements mean your general contractor's initial quoted price should only be considered an estimate and not a fixed price. It can fluctuate until the scope has been completed and the final invoices arrive from the subcontractor.

In reality, the general contractor will invoice at the end of a particular project phase or milestone for actual materials and labor used, plus overheads and a profit margin for themselves. A responsible contractor should be skilled at estimating probable costs, minimizing surprises, and keeping aligned with their original estimates. A cost-plus mode, however, protects them from doing unpaid work and buying unused materials. With careful supervision, it can also protect you from paying for things you don't need and provides the most fair and accurate way to execute your project.

SCHEDULING AND BUDGETING

For larger or institutional projects, you may be able to work to a guaranteed maximum price agreement. This type of agreement is sometimes referred to as a lump sum agreement, and ensures everyone works to an agreed overall price. This is considered a high risk for general contractors, and they price the work accordingly. It may be that a guaranteed price ultimately means a higher price for you than a cost-plus model, but you enjoy the confidence that comes from a fixed budget, which may be necessary for a payment structure, corporate policy, board of directors, etc.

Working to a fixed cost in this way does assume the project will run completely as planned. This is highly unlikely, and changes mean extra work that will come at a cost. As a result, change orders should be understood and are the mechanism used for unforeseen circumstances, or 'scope creep', where you add items to your wish list during construction or come across unplanned situations. These may also require the architect to create new drawings and documents for the contractors to perform this work. With a fixed-price contract, an effective change order process means work outside the original contract can be managed effectively with minimal stress. It pays to take care to understand exactly what the change order is covering and how the change order came to be. A change order should never be a surprise. Your general contractor ought to be timely in communications and you will be able to approve all additional work, or not, prior to it commencing.

If you are carrying a contingency in your budget, this may be used to cover the cost of any change orders. However, by their nature, they are difficult to predict, and the list of unplanned changes can grow quickly without due care.

Understanding the terms 'pre-construction', 'value engineering', and 'pro forma'

Projects can initially seem limited by cost, but if this occurs, the problem is due to a mismatch between project prices and costs assembled, your wish list, and your available funds. To avoid stopping a project before it starts, it is important to explain your goals to your contractor in detail and let them use their expertise to calculate costs and prices as determined by the market and their local subcontractors. There is no magic in this process; it is a case of working through the pricing phases and making fairly rudimentary calculations. Once you have a figure, it can be adjusted by reducing the scope of work or compromising on the quality of fit and finish. This negotiation is key to settling on an agreed project budget.

This phase of activity is often known as pre-construction (pre-con) work. This describes a pricing effort during the design phases to adjust the design to match the funds available for the project. There are many general contractors that offer this service on a

SCHEDULING AND BUDGETING

contractual or hourly basis. Through completing this task, a general contractor will gain valuable insight into your project and objectives, which could also prove to be valuable for executing the project. Otherwise, specialist third-party estimating companies can also be employed to assist in pre-construction pricing. The advantage to having a general contractor partner perform pricing early in the project is to directly inform the design before costly rounds of changes become necessary. Local construction industry knowledge and experience in similar projects are very important for anyone involved in pre-construction pricing.

'Value engineering' is a term that describes a repricing required after an adjustment to a completed final design. It has come to mean 'cost-saving' and is often undertaken to find out if there is a cheaper, quicker way to solve an architectural problem after the fact. It is typically implemented at a time in the project that is not conducive to major design changes and can disrupt or upset the energy or flow of a project as it requires the architect to revisit a design they had considered complete. This is also typically done once most of the design fee has been spent, so changes are often more superficial to avoid the need to expensively redo major design elements on the project.

The third term you should be familiar with is the budget pro forma. This typically refers to a spreadsheet containing the project costs and metrics. This may mean presenting costs against loan terms and the project's duration and schedule. It can also mean presenting simple costs for each discipline on the project on an ongoing basis. Whatever the pro forma contains, it is important that it is in an understandable format that is easy to use. A good pro forma makes it straightforward to understand the cost and schedule implications of project decisions. If well maintained, a pro forma will make sure you are informed and equipped to choose how, where, and when you spend your time and money. This is also the best way to see the entire project scope at one time. After reviewing your pro forma, you should be able to prioritize the elements that are most important, while not losing track of the essentials.

Thinking differently about cost

Our North American mentality seems to focus intently on costs, often before any thought has gone into the design process and establishing a project's overall goals and objectives. The experience of those who live, work, or spend time in the resulting project is surely more important than complaining over dollars. In reality, however, everything is related. Of course, we all want everything all at once, and at the lowest possible cost, but each project will have a unique mixture of ingredients. Cost, design, and experience exist together, but they will vary in different ratios with a specific focus from project to project. Architecturally, the focus is always on design with the intent to achieve a new client-specific experience, while considering level of fit and finish for durability at a reasonable cost. These factors often pull the project in opposing directions that need to be defined and reconciled with your architect before thinking about your budget.

That's not to say the budget isn't important, but putting it first can miss the point of the experience that well-considered and designed architecture will deliver. If finding the lowest cost is truly the primary objective, it is best to be transparent about your motivations and accept that some design professionals will struggle to find the right fit for your project.

In writing this, I am aware that finances are often an emotional subject we generally don't enjoy talking about. Try asking your friends and family about their salaries and see how that goes. A construction project can suffer from similar coyness. As it involves a very large capital expenditure, it becomes an inherently stressful endeavor. However, it needn't be. As mentioned earlier, starting with the most appropriate financing model is essential. It pays to get specific, be prepared, and be transparent about how the project is to be funded.

You should definitely inform the architect and general contractor of your financial objectives. They should be aware of how this impacts the project schedule and deadlines. Once the project scope is defined, you should be able to find appropriate financial institutions. It's worth talking to at least three lenders from small local businesses, through regional players to large national institutions. Each of these financial options will approach lending for these projects differently. They may all have approximately the same rates and terms, but it's worth digging a little deeper to compare their processes and fine print. Will they slow your project down because they will need to inspect the project every time you want to pay your contractor? Will they have contractual requirements that may turn some contractors or their subcontractors away? Will your lender understand the local AHJs and how the permitting process works? It's a very good idea to go into how the project is organized and have these aspects figured out and agreed on early. This will limit surprises and keep the project moving as smoothly as possible.

ARCHITECT'S ANECDOTE:
Working with your lender

We completed a project in Chicago with a client whose lender had given them a loan rate lock. The terms of this bank arrangement, however, seemed to be a moving target and very opaque, and we did not have enough of this information or understanding to include in the design process as it affects timeline.

We had introduced the client to a contractor that we knew and had great experiences with in the past. They were particularly helpful with pre-construction assistance during the early design phases of the project. We were excited.

Things, however, began to go awry when the lender requirements and timeline changed. This got worse as the lender began to dictate the project schedule. The client was initially told they had ninety days to provide pricing, which turned into forty-five and, finally, landed on thirty days.

These lender requirements proved so difficult to meet that the design process, pre-con phase, and costing suffered. Thanks to this lender, additional time was required to realign the general contractor with the project design to iron out pricing later in the process, out of natural order. This was all driven by a lender who did not understand the early phases of the project's definition and a client who did not communicate all of the elements with the project team.

Considering costs over your project's lifecycle

Depending on the scale and scope of your project, it can take anything from two months to a year to complete the design phase sufficiently to price. The average time for the design process of a typical residential project is ten to twenty weeks from inception through to the end of the initial design phase; however, this is a very personal process to each individual architecture firm, and is a direct result of the project size and complexity. The deliverable of this phase is normally schematic drawings that give an overview of the project in sufficient detail to start the pricing process. Most reputable general contractors can take schematic design drawings and provide a price for you in two to four weeks. This will often be an estimate for the purposes of establishing a projected baseline budget that corresponds to your wish list.

This may align with your expectations and available funds, which means the project can move on to the next phase. It may not, and the project may come full circle. You will then need to have a meaningful conversation with your architect about all the decisions and choices that have been made to date.

Let us assume that all is well, and your initial price estimate is within the limits you set yourself. How do you calculate if saying yes, greenlighting the project, and making the investment in the build will pay off? The answer is to consider a return over the project's full lifecycle for you and your family. Every project will have a lifecycle and it's important to have this discussion upfront. Each project type, be it a house, an office, a retail project, or an institutional project will vary. For now, let's consider a straightforward residential project built for the owners to occupy. We can immediately discount turning over the home for sale or to another new owner. That value proposition is quite straightforward, and you could base any decision-making on the likelihood of making a profit.

If you are planning for longer-term use, you could use the current real estate value as a baseline target, but

SCHEDULING AND BUDGETING

what if you plan to live in the home for ten, twenty, or fifty years? If you are building a home to live in, you perhaps should base investment decisions on future real estate projections. This is notoriously difficult and represents a significant risk. It also ignores the fact that properties, and homes specifically, are more than investments. Can you put a price on years of living in your dream spaces? At the end of the day, only you can decide what that is worth.

Architecture has the power to create new and wonderful experiences but it is important to maintain an awareness of where the cost lies in any project. Time and an efficient schedule are also of great importance. There is an intrinsic relationship and balance between these three factors in each project. The three may ebb and flow during the project, directed through dialogue between you and your team. It's important to maintain this dialogue and make sure that the architect and general contractor remain on the same page. Understanding how to speak to both about money so that they are aware of your position is essential. Keeping a project on budget so you are not out of pocket depends on it.

Practical thoughts on scheduling and budgeting

1. Have a frank discussion about your wish list, how quickly you need the project finished, and how much you want to spend early in the

project. Be prepared to compromise as to how these three factors balance, one of these will want to drive the project.

2. For a typical residential or renovation project, include a contingency of 3–5% to the budget for unforeseen circumstances and possible project changes. This is an easy way to lower project stress levels.

3. Remember that 'pre-con' work during the design process will achieve a more accurate price. This will lead to a smoother project for all parties.

4. Have a conversation about contractor estimates, contract models, and ways to manage any changes early in the project. Once you understand these, choose a path and stick to it.

5. Maintain your own pro forma throughout the project. It will allow you to have a clear, confident understanding about what is happening, what is being spent, and how that compares to initial estimates.

3
Communicating During The Project

You've reached a point where you're happy with the design, the team, project costs, and the design and project schedule. We ought to pause here and discuss a vital part of the process that is sometimes forgotten at great cost. Communication.

Communication is the most important aspect to any project. Good architects are generally effective communicators as well as being technically proficient, experienced, and organized. If they can't explain their actions, the project will struggle. This is a two-way street, though. It is worth considering if you, as the client, are a strong communicator. What do you do well? What could you improve on?

This is important, because effective communication from all sides will result in a far stronger project and a better experience for the whole project team, including yourself. You should expect project updates from your architect and general contractor that are timely and sufficiently detailed to answer any of your questions. Your part of the deal is to respond clearly and promptly. The best way to ensure everyone works together well is to agree on a communication method early in the project.

Using email, text, and apps

While it's true that communication methods ought to be tailored to each project, most professionals will have a proven methodology. It is not unusual, for example, for a project team to propose regular updates by email, simply because that is what they are used to. It is important, however, that you feel able to challenge these practices and have your particular wishes recorded and recognized.

What is reasonable? Email, text, apps, and telephone are the primary means of communication for much of the professional world these days. Email is the most common and allows both sides the opportunity to share thoughts, share information, and facilitate effective decisions.

A response time of twenty-four hours for emails feels realistic for most projects. If a response takes longer than twenty-four hours, it may be because the answer needs some research or input from third parties, but this should at least be acknowledged with a response that the answer is forthcoming.

It is worth noting that email is not a great way to have a dialogue. It is still best suited to formal exchanges. Long email chains of back-and-forth chat soon become difficult to manage and key pieces of information can get lost in the dialogue. Before sending an email, it is worth spending time checking that you have created a well-composed response that provides the required information clearly and concisely, responding to all questions asked. The takeaway here should be to respect people's time and understand what the sender needs from you. There are, of course, instances when picking up the phone to ask questions directly might be the better means of communication. This can often save time by 'cutting to the chase'.

Texting is a newer means of quick, less formal communication that is often used between contractors and their sub-contracted tradespeople. It is so new that the professional world is still figuring out how best to use it. Sending a text comes with an inherent expectation of an immediate response and it can be better than email to have a dialogue. This is good and bad. It is perfect for simple questions that require a yes or no response. It is why the majority of texts seem to be about confirming meeting times and locations. Their informality means that it's not the place for making decisions – especially ones that could impact the cost or schedule. If this is the case, the text should be accompanied by an email for recording the information and any possible decisions.

Your project team may also use project management software or an app to communicate. These often streamline processes and can be very helpful. If they do, make sure that full access is available to you to view records throughout the project. If texts or an app are used on the project, it is probably worth following up any important messages by email to ensure a more considered response is recorded. Over the years, email has become the default primary communication channel for many construction projects. Advances in message chains, search functions, and the organization of subject threads have been combined with better practices by most users. When paired with a large file-sharing method for the exchange of drawings and presentations, email is certainly sufficient as a formal means of communication. It also provides a digital paper trail, that can be very helpful along the project timeline to retrace decisions or a specific conversation in time. It is best to save communications with your architect and general contractor on a regular basis during the project and keep them in a safe place and backed-up with digital and paper records.

Typically, projects slow down when communication is poor. It becomes hard to make decisions if you don't have all the information you need to hand where

COMMUNICATING DURING THE PROJECT

and when it is required. This is increasingly difficult to manage, because our world is moving ever faster. Ironically, perhaps, the constant communication we have access to means it is harder to control information. Projects inevitably require different elements to be covered at the same time by different people. Managing these overlaps and communicating complex positions can be challenging for the design team and general contractor, but it is their job to keep you abreast of everything. A little understanding, however, goes a long way.

The most important lesson from this section is to make sure that you have consistent, clear communication with your architect and general contractor and that appropriate methods are discussed early in your process and followed through with.

It is important for you to have your own digital and physical filing system for your project. If necessary, you can have your architect talk you through this. Architects are generally very organized with their files – they need to be, given the thousands of files they work with. They should be able to guide you through setting up a filing system to keep track of all the incoming and outgoing pieces of information that will occur throughout your project.

These are very important records that should be kept. You may need to refer back to them at any point over the lifecycle of the project and property.

Making decisions

You will be required to make many decisions during the course of your project. This is a long process – some decisions will be easy and quick, while others may be difficult and require much more thought and information. And with the duration of the project, many decisions can be hard for anyone to keep track of. To help, it is important to be on the same page with the project team and comfortable with the flow of information. This will keep the process moving as smoothly as possible. During the project, floor plans, elevations, building sections, renderings, and other drawings, images, and deliverables will be created to communicate ideas for the project. These documents will be presented to you throughout the project, and you will be asked for feedback and decisions.

It is, therefore, essential to understand basic architectural drawings. These are straightforward once you know what they mean, what to look for, and how to read them. They are a graphic language used to communicate to the project team what to execute on your project. You may be asked to choose a preference between options.

If these drawings and other documents do not make sense, you need to raise this with your architect. Without the facts, you cannot make educated decisions. Do not be afraid to ask for help interpreting and reading any information you are given. Learn what is important, what to look for, and how to understand these documents.

The design team will quickly become intimately knowledgeable about your project. It can be easy for them to assume that you are keeping pace, so they may provide too little information or skip over important items by moving you too quickly through the process. If you feel this is the case, have a conversation about slowing the process down. It is important that you understand everything that is necessary to make the best decisions. All projects require a constant flow of effective decision-making to keep on schedule.

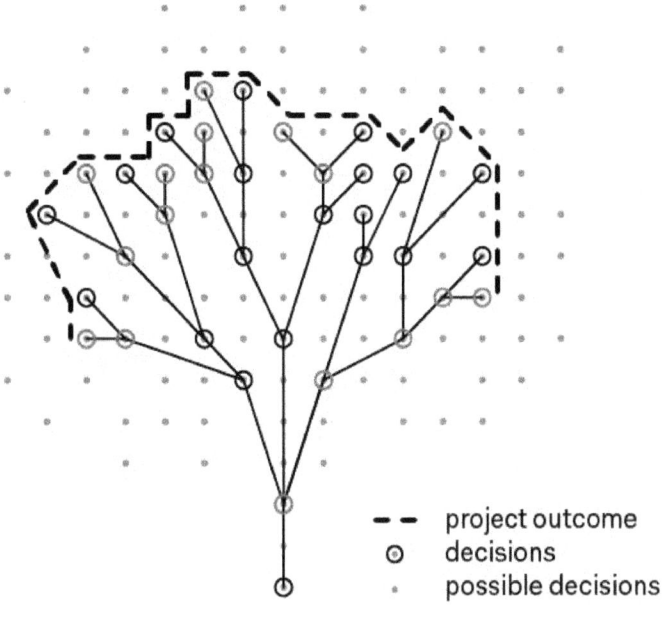

– –   project outcome
 ⊙   decisions
 ·   possible decisions

Decision tree

Decisions are what drive projects forward from iteration to iteration and from phase to phase. From when the architect begins to define the project, including all the features on your wish list, through to the general contractor's detailed input, there are many decision points and milestones for you, as the client, to handle. You will be given countless opportunities to review and approve the next steps. Your agreement with the architect may stipulate a certain number of revisions or rounds of changes with each phase. This should be clear from the beginning of the project. Constant reiterating the same point or revising drawings slows the project down and creates stress and anxiety. It is important that you make firm, clear, and proactive decisions. This will help the project keep a reasonable pace, reduce stress and anxiety, and keep the financial aspects of the project in order. Architects should be in tune with their client's pressure points too, and it's fair to have conversations about this to make sure that the process can be adjusted as required. It is in everyone's interest for you to have a positive project experience.

The takeaway for the decision-making aspect of your project is to work with your architect and, subsequently, general contractor to formalize a system for decision-making. How will questions be asked? How will decisions be communicated and recorded? Decisions are part of the regular communication between the architect, the client, and general contractor, so it is important they don't get missed in general project chatter. It is important that decisions are flagged and made apparent to everyone. For the project to have the best outcome possible, your opinions, and any actions that result from them, need to be clear to the whole team.

Setting project goals

You should have kicked off the project definition phase of any activity with a clear starting statement that shares your overall goal. The project scope and storyboard document should define these further. However, it is worth taking a moment to check that your goals are clear and consistent. There are four primary areas to address:

1. **Experience:** What will the end product feel like to live in or use?
2. **Design:** What will the end product look like?
3. **Financial:** How is the project being paid for and how much should the finished project be worth?
4. **Time:** How long will the end product take to build?

These are only headline examples and a starting point. There may be others that are specific to you or your circumstances. The important point here is to make sure that, as a minimum, these four are communicated early in the project and are maintained as targets during the project's duration. They may evolve, but goals that become moving targets without reason or adequate communication can be difficult to accommodate and manage. They create added pressure on any project. Let's look at each in turn.

Experiential goals

What experiences will the finished project provide? How will the building or project host home or work life? Architecture is constantly evaluated through the experiences of people using the spaces and buildings we design. Improving the lives of residents or workers or visitors is one of the most important objectives for any architect. As a client, it is important this way too. What do you want to achieve? How do you want users of your new project to feel mentally and physically? By designing and arranging our spaces and selecting the materials and finishes, fixtures, and equipment, architects create holistic ensembles of pieces and parts that work in concert together. Each project is a bespoke invention, a new solution to the client's situation. It is an opportunity to do things better than other buildings. You can, and should, consider this desire to change life for the better with your project. You'll get the best from your architect that way.

Design goals

What design elements are important? When writing the project narrative concept statement and assembling the presentation of precedents into the storyboard with your architect, think about the different areas of the project and where the focus should be. Are there areas that stand out as more important than the rest? For some, it may be the primary bedroom and bathroom. For many others, it's the kitchen, living, and dining room. For commercial clients, it may be the entrance, reception, and client-facing areas. The staff wellness and breakroom may be a priority. It is very important for your architect to understand your priorities. Difficult decisions around where and how to spend the investment available for these projects are inevitable. It is helpful for you and the project team to be aligned and clear design goals make this easier for everyone.

Financial goals

The investment available to the project should be clear. The financial aspect is no different from any other goals of the project, and the more transparent and franker you can be, the better. The design and construction process can be adjusted to respond to your circumstances. If acquiring a loan, for example, tell your architect what kind of loan you have and how it will work. What are the deliverables and timetables that your lender requires for the project? They should be reflected in your upfront project goals, as discovering they are not in sync once the project is underway will cause friction. Rigid lender processes can work against best practices given your project's other goals. If possible, it is useful to involve your architect and, possibly, general contractor (if one is on board at this point) to help give feedback on the loan criteria and its impacts on the design and construction process. Paying back the loan, of course, needs careful consideration. You should always remember the value of the finished project is an important goal too.

Time goals

In some cases, the project schedule is more important than the goals above. For all its complexities, the financial investment that a project requires can be less important than completing a project on a specific date. Hard-moving dates, family holiday expectations, office deadlines, or commercial sales cycles are often non-negotiable. If this applies to your project, it is important to communicate this from the early stages of engagement with your team. Often dramatically called a 'drop-dead' completion date, the entire project team will need to be aware and on board with this, as it will shape plans and decision-making from day one. If you aren't under time pressure, it is still worth considering a time goal for your project. Even an open-ended completion date benefits from a vague target, otherwise you'll continually be set back by more urgent deadlines. Whatever your time goal, it is important to build some contingency into the schedule to accommodate unknown circumstances that may arise. There are so many moving parts and parties that it can be difficult to keep all in alignment right to the finish line.

A clear goal communicated to the whole team helps keep everyone on track.

The language of your project goals is translated into architecture, design, and construction objectives by the project team. The only way this happens is through transparency. First, you define what you want with the architect, then make sure that your project team understands and includes them in their processes. These goals and objectives should be tracked throughout the duration of the project to make sure that they are being maintained. These projects are time-consuming, with long durations and many factors that need to be aligned. It is easy for them to drift off target. Your successful project will employ a process keeping you at the center, managing all of these factors in a manner that you understand.

Aligning your personal finances

As building a property is likely to mark a significant capital investment for you, it is worth pausing briefly to talk about personal finances. We should all strive to have sound financial goals. A person's financial situation is often a very private affair. People don't seem to share financial information often, so financial goals can feel as if we are all sort of walking around chasing a ghost of some sort – partially consisting of one's past, family experiences, the information gained with a partner, other factors, influences from your job, and perhaps from an investment adviser or an accountant. Piece all of this together and it can be confusing, to say the least, but you need to get a good overview of how all your finances fit together before taking the leap into a major project. Hopefully, this book serves as a primer for the architecture and construction parts of the picture at the very least.

When putting construction projects together it can be incredibly helpful to figure out how to use 'other' people's money for your project rather than your own. This will involve researching and understanding market loan products and having conversations with various lenders, as we've discussed earlier in the book. You may want to have a construction loan that can be converted into a conventional loan at the time of completion. This is often your best avenue for a project. There are plenty of other lending products that function the same way. Architects are not experts in the lending world, but we do know that it takes a long time to build an investment portfolio and to spend it on a project seems counterproductive when other financial vehicles exist to fund these types of projects.

If you are looking to borrow money, it is important to get your credit cleaned up. If this means setting up alerts through your own bank or paying for a subscription from a credit bureau, it is worth it to make sure that your credit score is as high as possible. Then it is always worth sitting down with your banker and figuring out all the best steps to getting your finances where you will need them to be before deciding to launch into a project. This could take years to execute, as the credit bureaus seem to be some of the slowest-reacting agencies that have such importance in our lives. However, it is worth being patient. If you are going to take on a construction project in your life and need financing, good credit makes things a lot easier. Work on it regularly.

Whatever method you choose to fund the project, it pays to separate your emotions from the financial aspects. This can be impossible at times, but you must try. During any architecture and construction project, emotions will be running high, especially if costs are heading upwards rather than downwards. If you're prepared, good decisions are well within your reach and will keep you in your comfort zone. It pays to keep a calm, level head.

I am not a financial adviser, but will conclude this section on finances by suggesting you leave your money where it is invested until you retire. Keeping a construction project as its own financial vehicle, separate from your other investments and interests, can save you a lot of heartache. If it feels like you need to liquidate investments to do your project, this can be an indicator that it is not the right time for you and more planning is necessary. Take a step back and re-evaluate the entire position. Speak to your accountant, investment adviser, mentor, or your friends and family to get an unemotional perspective about the situation.

Practical thoughts on project communication

1. It is important to establish clear methods of regular communication on your project. This communication will need to happen between you, your architect, and your contractor. It's also important that this communication is allowed to overlap and be as open as possible. Try to be inclusive and keep everyone on the same page.

2. Agree on a plan which means communication happens regularly during the project. Use email, text, and apps carefully to organize and record decisions and milestones.

3. Decision-making is vital. Your architect and contractor will need you to make firm, clear, and consistent decisions throughout your project.

4. Make sure you understand design drawings sufficiently to make educated decisions. Ask for help if you need it.

5. Make sure to be clear about your project's experience, design, financial, and scheduling goals. Be realistic. These goals want to be aligned with your finances and this all needs to be transparent. Once set, try not to change these positions as moving targets will delay your project and cause friction.

PART TWO
DESIGNING YOUR PROJECT

4
Getting Started

We are roughly halfway through the book and all we've talked about is defining the project. We haven't even started designing yet. As the client, this is as it should be. The more time, effort, and thought you put into your project ahead of time, the better. Once things get started, opportunities to change your mind come at a cost.

The good news is designing projects is what architects love to do. They enjoy the profession for the moments they can use design to make new ideas real – taking something from the page to a solid, tangible building. Solving spatial challenges and using materials in a creative manner with design is a very rewarding process.

Architects think three-dimensionally and on different scales very quickly. They problem-solve through iteration and experimentation, which is liberating. It is, however, a time-consuming endeavor, based on years of experience. When initially speaking with architects, this is why it is worth digging into how they work. You ought to discuss how much time they spend on projects, while asking to see examples of actual projects. You should talk through what was involved in the different phases of work. Research, drawing, modeling, managing, and coordination are all part of the package, but differ from design. It is design that motivates most architects. Design is both the professional and personal process architects understand and use.

It is not difficult to get architects to open up and discuss their processes. It might be more difficult to shut some of us up. However, it is a passion, and you'll have a smoother working relationship with your architect if you understand this and let them enjoy the job!

Understanding the role of your architect

Your architect will do a lot of work for your project. A huge amount of work. Even describing it feels like a daunting task. The key fact to remember is your architect is your primary advocate on your project. When an architect first hears of a project, it ought to feel

GETTING STARTED

exciting. The initial meeting should feel like a creative beginning that can be made real – something that resonates with both parties. Given their experience and professional background, your architect should see a path through the project to the end. A good, engaged, and passionate architect should know where you need to get to, even if you don't yet. They should be ten, twenty, or thirty steps ahead, wanting to figure out everything on the project as if it's a puzzle being assembled in their mind. It's this skill that an architect brings to the team.

The discipline an architect ought to bring along with this creativity is a well-defined and documented process that means you can see it step-by-step too. A successful project happens when the architect's design process allows for a calm, collected, and sensible decision-making process. It is when the process is led astray or there is an influence that occurs out of sync or misaligned with the project that problems occur.

Your architect and any consultants they use should be able to clearly define and explain their individual scopes and estimate the timelines that this work will require. Your architect will take you through various project phases that are appropriate for your individual project. These may not be the same project to project. Depending on the project starting point, goals, and objectives, the project phases can be adjusted to respond to and accommodate your circumstances. Generally, however, the architect's scope should be

SPEAKING ARCHITECTURE

split into two. Initially, they will define their clients' projects and the necessary architect's and engineer's responses. We've discussed this in the first half of the book. Once that is complete and agreed upon, they will typically move on to clear phases of work that respond to the client's individual situation and project.

These phases are: research and discovery; programming; concept; schematic design; design development; permit; construction documents; construction.

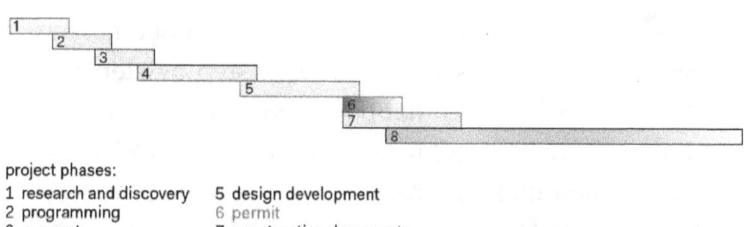

project phases:
1 research and discovery
2 programming
3 concept
4 schematic design
5 design development
6 permit
7 construction documents
8 construction

The phases of work

These phases may encompass all appropriate work your architect (and general contractor) will deliver to complete your project, and they may adjust as necessary – for instance, your project may not require all of these phases. This should be determined with your architect at the beginning of your process. The key is appropriate work. It is important to remember the architect is not working to their own agenda.

GETTING STARTED

They are not even working directly for you, per se. Once the project is defined, and set in motion, it becomes its own entity, with its own energy. Your architect ought to work in the project's best interests at all times. They ask questions directly to 'the project' and look for responses. It is an architect's role to decide what is and what isn't appropriate. They ask 'the project' if a certain design move is warranted and then see the resulting outcome. This means good architects are not always in the business of giving clients what they want all the time. They always prioritize their projects and develop relationships with them in a manner that means emotional and irrational decisions are reduced or removed. Importantly, this is most effective with a well-defined project where objectives have been clearly established at the onset.

The architect is the advocate that balances the project's needs with your desires in an unbiased manner. Their role is guiding all parties to the best results as they simultaneously manage all aspects of the project. The collective stakeholders on the project will no doubt input their views, but it is the architect that conducts the complex series of overlapping layers to keep the project on track. Communication and organization skills are often as important as technical skills here, so it is vital that you feel comfortable with your architect playing this central role.

Signing an agreement with your architect

The architectural contract or agreement is, on the face of it, relatively straightforward. There are only a few ways to look at any professional service, after all. Your architect will spend time on your project and your agreement describes the mechanism by which, they will be remunerated for that time. This can run to thousands of hours on a single project. For instance, completing the architectural scope for a new house from beginning to conclusion can be anywhere between 300 hours and 2,500 hours. As an aside, one year is 2,080 hours based on a forty-hour week. The takeaway here isn't that an architect only needs 300 hours to complete an entire new house project. The point is that there is an enormous swing. Every project is different, and its circumstances need to be fully understood and clearly defined, hence all the preparation work upfront.

Most architects are invested in their work and want to do the best job they possibly can. They also need to balance the project with the client's expectations and available investment. Things can, and do, change too. With so many moving parts, any architect's agreement needs to have a mechanism for accommodating the fact that projects evolve. It pays to have an understanding and flexible working relationship knowing that demands on time and resources become clearer after early project phases are complete.

GETTING STARTED

With the changing nature of projects in mind, architects typically work a few different ways. These can be broadly split into three categories:

1. A fixed fee

2. Hourly rates

3. A combination of the two

If it's a fixed fee, it is often based on a percentage of the overall hard costs of construction. This will be based on the architect's experience of similar project expectations, and will likely include a contingency figure. With a fixed fee, asking for work to be repeated or reviewed because you change your mind or circumstances alter will normally come as an additional cost. It is important you agree on how changes are to be managed and paid for with your architect.

An architect can also simply tell you how many hours they've spent on a task and ask to be reimbursed. This is typically on a monthly basis. They still ought to be able to estimate a maximum fee based on a percentage of the hard costs of construction for planning and budgeting purposes. You might be lucky and the architect uses less than the predicted hours, but you may overspend. A good, reliable architect should minimize any surprises.

Your architect may also vary their fee approach depending on the phase of work. They may prefer to be reimbursed on an hourly basis for phases that have a heavy or open-ended design and decision-making process. Once the project is defined and it's a matter of completing all the technical and coordinating work, the design team can provide a more accurate timeline and the fee can be fixed. All architects approach their fees differently – there are industry guidelines, but no set rules.

A billing conversation should happen at the beginning of any project, as you must understand exactly what you have signed up for in any working relationship. Architectural drawings will form part of the discussion with your architect. They are the work product that will get your project constructed. It is important to agree on the appropriate number of design iterations or changes for each project element. Redrawing or amending them takes up billable hours. As a client, it can prove costly to fret over small details and change your mind too often.

Not all drawings are equal. Every architect approaches this part of their craft differently, but they will generally produce drawings in a series that builds in information as layers that become more detailed as they develop. The drawings are the graphic representation of the project, which represents its goals and objectives. They are submitted to regulators (AHJs) for approval, and they describe what is to be built by the general contractor and their subcontractors. The project agreement with your architect ought to, therefore, include a drawing list, or matrix, defined by phase. This will allow you to follow your architect's processes and track their work. It will also give you an understanding of the amount of work required to complete the project from start to finish. This is a good conversation for everyone to have at the beginning of the project, even before signing a contract. Some architects are well organized and will be prepared to have this conversation. Others may not be. The drawing matrix from the architect's agreement could also be included in your general contractor agreement as the specific set of drawings to be executed. The handover marks a major milestone in the project.

Many architects have their own contracts and agreements that they will want to use, but it might be in your best interests to form your own. When approached this way, you will feel better informed and feel better equipped to deal with any dispute. Also, if you develop your own agreement with your attorney, they will already know all about it. It is worth noting that the American Institute of Architects (AIA) has done tremendous work making template contracts available for purchase. They might also be available through your architect. Once purchased, an attorney can customize the contract for your specific project, adding language to cover the architect's and general contractor's scope, schedules, finances, and so on.

Whatever approach you choose to create an agreement, it should confirm that your architect will create a set of drawings and documents for an agreed amount of money. The drawings and documents apply to your specific project, at that specific time, and for that specific location. These documents will be created through various phases of work, with agreed rounds of iteration to finalize the design scope and match your goals and objectives. It is important to be clear you are not buying a set of drawings. Your architect, or any other design professional you work with, retains the copyright of the material. This means if you have plans for any design beyond the immediate project, please discuss them with your team before moving forward.

It's important to have an agreement in place with your architect and understand costs and payment structures, the time allotted or scheduled for the work, and the drawings and documents that will be used for your project. These are the parameters that define the relationship between the two of you. If all is clear and transparently written into your contract, it will lead to a smoother, more successful, and happier process.

Understanding your architect's work

We touched on the architect's phases of work in the preceding section, but will now dive into more detail. Each phase of work should be tailored to your specific project and organized to maximize effectiveness and efficiency. The phases move from the general to

GETTING STARTED

the specific. The initial phases of the project should begin conceptually or broadly and include lots of client participation. They are the phases where you will be asked to make key decisions and approve work before moving into the subsequent phase. It is important to make sure your architect doesn't get too far into the process without approved direction. Heading down an undesirable path without checking in with you could cause unnecessary, expensive, and time-consuming redesign and redrawing.

When the project begins, it is worth checking that you understand the deliverables the team will be working on and presenting to you. Your architect will use drawings, diagrams, renderings, and other imagery to communicate your next steps and options. The process works best with swift feedback and approval, so understanding how to read and interpret basic drawings, imagery, and documents plays a large part. The architect can adjust their communication style to suit the project needs to a degree, but may be unable to accommodate specific requirements. Again, it is important to discuss your requirements upfront.

Architectural drawing comprehension is not common, so you should not feel remotely embarrassed about asking for help. Although they are 'easier' to read, it can be challenging to review 3D renderings, artists' impressions, and photo-realistic graphics. Especially early in the project, it is important to remember architects are presenting possibilities rather than finalized ideas. We discussed the dangers of this earlier in the book. The best advice is to ask your architect to see the drawings, renderings, and documents they have created from a project that is similar to yours in scope prior to starting work. You can talk through what was involved with making them and how they were used.

Your architect is here to help you at every phase of the design and construction activity. They will want to be a resource and your advocate. They will have been through the process of delivering a project many times before. If you have the right conversations at the beginning of the project and find the required alignments, you'll succeed.

Understanding contract documents

We have discussed deliverables, but they are such an important topic that they deserve further discussion. In the simplest terms, the construction documents are the architectural drawings and specifications that are used to build your project, prepared by the architect and their consultants for the fee in the project agreement. Later in this chapter, we will discuss all the variations and structures that architects use to achieve this.

Before then, I propose taking a slight tangent, because this is the right moment to discuss copyright and design ownership. What does this mean? How does it affect the project? What does it mean to you? The short answer is that it often has no effect at all. The nuance here is that the architect technically retains ownership of the design and the copyright to the design. Clients sometimes have the misconception that they are buying the drawings or design for the fee paid to the architect. This is simply not the case unless specifically written into the contract.

The design, drawings, specifications, renderings, etc, form the contract documents, and are the architect's intellectual property (IP). All you are technically paying for is the right to use the drawings or design to construct the project at a specific time and location. If you want more than this and can see opportunities for future use of the design elsewhere, it is important you raise this with your architect ahead of time. They are unlikely to say no, but they will want to be correctly compensated.

Architect's drawings vary greatly from company to company, project to project, and in some cases, client to client. Architects that work primarily designing public spaces or office buildings, for example, might not be the best fit for a house project. However good they may be, they may not have relevant experience. This also ripples down to the types of drawings they make and how they make them.

Architectural drawings, renderings, and specifications come in many forms. The general term 'blueprint' is still used more often than necessary and is a legacy term for a basic set of architectural drawings or prints. These drawings are printed on large sheets of paper and bound together to make a set. These initial drawings are submitted with your building permit application. They provide basic dimensions, specification information, and the overall look of your project. They are also used by the general contractor and their subcontractors to calculate their prices and then start building. They are two-dimensional, depicting plans, elevations, sections, and other details. The drawing sets will also include notes, diagrams, schedules, and specifications. These specifications (often shortened to specs), can be contained in a separate document that is read together with the drawing set. Your local AHJ will also require certain drawings and specifications before assessing a project and approving any building permit application. The building department will define what drawings need to be submitted when dealing with life and safety requirements. I have been using two terms: construction documents and contract documents. For the purpose of this book, these terms can be thought of as interchangeable, the nuance being that contract documents are those drawings and documents that specifically form the part of the agreement between you and your GC for pricing and building your project.

As well as delivering these as a statutory minimum, architects will provide drawings to communicate the project's goals and objectives. These goals and

GETTING STARTED

objectives are unique to each project. There are many drawing conventions, and each project can, to a degree, define a graphic language of its own to communicate how it is to be constructed. Architects adjust the drawing and document deliverables on a project in response to their specific project brief.

As a result, the package of drawings and documents can be small and lean, or thick and comprehensive. Architects work with a spectrum of responses to a project's goals and objectives. A simple project, for example, might rely more heavily on a general contractor to interpret the goals and objectives and work directly with the client on design decisions. This may warrant a lean set of contract documents. If the goals and objectives are complex and detailed, however, the project will need a more comprehensive set of drawings and documents to give the general contractor so they have adequate information to price and build the desired vision.

If cost is driving your decision here, you need to have a conversation with your architect about the details. Lean documents might save you money upfront, but lead to more expense down the line.

Architects don't rely on drawings alone. They typically use presentations to communicate project ideas. A combination of floor plans, elevations, sections, and detailed drawings as well as renderings, visualizations, material palettes, etc, are used in these presentations. It is worth talking through each in turn.

Floor plans

Floor plans are drawings of the building cut parallel to the floor plane at 4ft off the floor. This is why windows and doors are visible, but elements such as clerestory windows and light fixtures are not. Furniture and other items can be included to test the spatial concepts of the project and to communicate the fit to the client. The purpose of a floor plan is to agree upon room dimensions and placement of windows, doors, and other main features.

Elevations

Exterior elevations are drawings that depict the outside of the building as though viewed straight on. They are not in perspective, which is the way the world appears to the human eye. Elevations flatten the view at right angles to simplify dimensions and descriptions. They are used to communicate heights, window and door placements, material choices, etc.

Interior elevations have the same concept as exterior, but are slightly more abstract as they are bound by the interior walls and do not show wall thickness. They can depict finishes, such as tile, millwork, case goods, lighting, electrical fixtures, and other details.

GETTING STARTED

Sections

Sections are further abstractions that 'cut' through the building at a specific point. They show wall thicknesses, as well as interior elevations in the background. Section drawings are used to help understand how project pieces connect. A building section will give a spatial sense or feeling from adjacent room to room, or even to the exterior. They may show how stairs and elevators work, for example. They can demonstrate how the interior connects to the exterior through windows, doors, and the wider structural system.

Details

Detailed drawings zoom in on smaller elements of the project. Details are used to determine how materials at a human scale are put together for the project. They can illustrate how reveals and trim of drywall, wood, stone, or tile might feel to the people that use the space. This is where many architects love to operate, and this conversation would be remiss to leave out the Mies van der Rohe quote: 'God is in the details.'[1]

The details and material usage can make or break a project. They represent the pieces of a building we see, feel, and touch every day. Unfortunately, they are often overlooked, misunderstood, and engineered out of projects. It cannot be stressed enough to be on

---

1 M van der Rohe, *Architectural Forum* (May 1958)

the same page as the architect about their approach to details. With a misaligned architect, they may not even exist in the way you want or are expecting.

Details are a great starting point for aligning project priorities and verifying the best match with a design professional. Asking the architect to see details from a previous project and have them walk through and explain how they work speaks volumes. You are looking for passion from drawings to the finished product. If there is an understanding and appreciation of details that matches yours, then it is a great sign. This part of the relationship is often overlooked, yet a lack of care over the details can ruin a project.

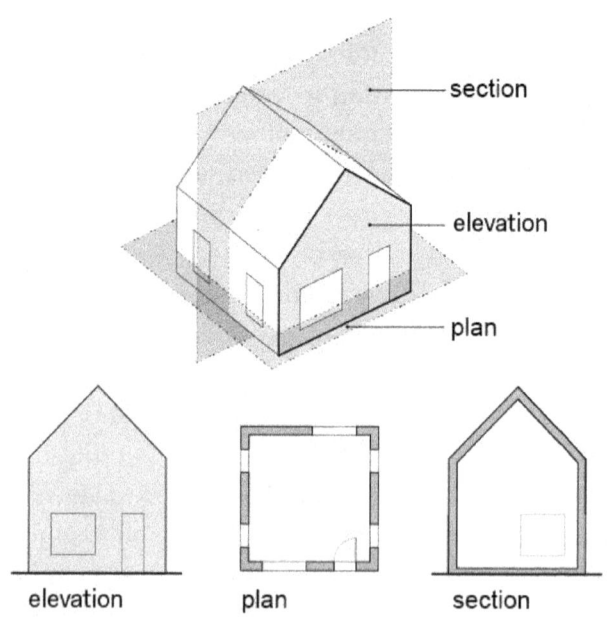

Plan, elevation, and section defined

In summary, it is important to make sure you are on the same page with your team when it comes to how drawings are managed throughout the project. If in doubt, ask for clarification.

Using 3D renderings

Renderings are images created of your project using three-dimensional computer modeling tools. These renders are further edited in software to finalize them for presentations. They seem to have become almost mandatory to convince clients of their project's viability and success. There has been a shift away from trusting the architect and working to understand two-dimensional drawings, to requiring three-dimensional imagery to see what a project will 'look like'. For architects, this is both exciting and detrimental. It is exciting because they can now use this tool to test design ideas spatially, but detrimental because the process can get stuck in an iterative cycle based on one image rather than the larger architectural ideas.

It is worth remembering that seeing and understanding three-dimensional space based on two-dimensional drawings is a skill that can be learned. Renderings are also not required for the AHJ or contractors. As a result, it is worth being sensitive about how the rendering process is used. The desire to see a finished image too soon can put unnecessary stress on your project without achieving a result. Is creating a three-dimensional image the best use of your architect's time? It might seem it in the short-term, but it is much better to let the process continue towards a complete drawing package uninterrupted.

Adding an interior designer to your project

Interior design is planning and supervising the design and execution of architectural interiors, including the specifying of furniture, fixtures (lighting, plumbing, etc), and equipment. This is sometimes shortened to FFE. The disciplines of architecture and interior design clearly overlap. Architects that are interested in the design of buildings and space to achieve a desired experience for the users are very interested in the interior scope of their projects too. When interviewing architects, it is worth asking what interior design services they provide, and how the fee for these services is structured. Some architectural practices are not interested in providing interior design services, but others do, and there are perhaps efficiencies and savings to be made by combining the two work scopes. Architects with interior design expertise will, for example, use furniture and other items they believe work best for the project.

Interior design often comes with a different fee structure than architecture, with interior design fees appearing lower at the onset. This is because interior designers use any purchases they make and add a margin to make up the fees. They may negotiate a 40% discount on an item of furniture but only pass 10–15% of that on to you. The remainder is retained as part of their fee. This still means purchasing furniture for less than buying items directly, but can add significantly to the interior designer's income. It is generally considered an advantageous arrangement all-round.

The architect and interior design delineation can be made anywhere you wish. Architects and interior designers have different viewpoints, and it is best to define these boundaries and expectations early in the process with your team. An interior designer's input can lead to scope creep, as it adds another opinion to the mix. Alternatively, another design professional on the project may add value. You will have to make a judgment.

Handling furniture, fixtures, and equipment (FFE)

The clearest interior design input is FFE. Furniture, fixtures, and equipment are the layers that people will see, touch, and feel. It is important to consider each of these aspects to make sure that they are all coordinated and working towards achieving the desired experience. Whether you need specialist help is up to you and your project.

'Furniture', for architects, often refers to anything on the interior of the building or home that is not attached to the walls, floor, or ceiling. There can be a gray area between millwork (a term for woodwork in a home such as doors, mantels, and shelving), casework (cabinets and storage), and furniture (tables, chairs, and so on). Many architects will design the millwork and casework elements for the project, particularly if they are fitted. For furniture, this will depend on the architect you are working with and the agreement you've come to regarding interiors. 'Fixtures' generally refers to decorative electrical fixtures and plumbing fixtures. We are talking about wall sconces, pendants, and toilets, sinks, medicine cabinets, and so on. 'Equipment' often refers to mechanical, electrical, and plumbing equipment in any home or building. This includes items such as your furnace, water heater, boilers, electric panels, and so on. It may also include your main kitchen appliances and other specialized equipment that is desired or necessary for your project. You may want to be heavily involved with some of these choices, while you may just want to be aware of others and confirm that the choices meet your expectations.

The FFE discussion should begin in the initial scope defining and costing phases. This is when the project will want to define the various pieces of the scope of the team members. For instance, it may make sense that your general contractor's mechanical subcontractor purchases and installs the equipment in their scope. This is most often the case with plumbing and electrical equipment as well, for example. However, some of this could either fall on you, the general contractor, or an interior design professional. What is your view on your lighting fixtures, kitchen appliances, or bathroom tile and fixtures? Who is the most appropriate person for these responsibilities? Who will have the greatest purchasing advantage? Who should own the installation and take responsibility for ensuring they are functional without holding up the schedule? This all needs to be assigned and agreed.

When purchasing FFE, there is always retail pricing, and then varying levels of industry discounts depending on all manner of factors. Interior design firms often work with set industry rates or negotiate special rates. General contractors will have relationships with suppliers that give them purchasing power as well. It is important to have these conversations early to align expectations with opportunities and make the best choices given the circumstances. Some FFE items can have long lead times, and some will require coordination on site and in your project. There is little point in having your bathroom tile and fixtures delivered until the plumbing installation is scheduled, for example. If you, as the client, take responsibility for purchasing some items, you will also take responsibility for that entire piece of work. You may be 'on the hook' for pieces missing in a complicated order and any delay to the installation and overall schedule. This may or may not be worth any perceived savings.

Coordinating FFE items can be challenging. If we return to your bathroom as an example, plumbing fixtures should be designed to work with the layout of finishes that are selected for your interior, such as tile, sinks, millwork, and other elements. These plumbing fixtures have rough valves that are installed in the walls long before the finishes and final plumbing trim are installed. Changing the locations or specifications of these rough plumbing valves is costly after finishes have been installed. These small details, however, are what make the difference between an average project and a great one.

Practical thoughts on working with your architect

1. It is important to understand what an architect does. If you aren't clear about the various drawings, images, diagrams, and documents that they create to complete your project, then ask.

2. Work with your architect to define their scope. Tailor this to your expectations, your objectives, and the reality of your project requirements. They need to match the unique circumstances of your project.

GETTING STARTED

3. Make certain that you have adequate contracts in place with both your architect and general contractor, and any other consultant hired directly. Use AIA templates and seek the counsel of an attorney for assistance during this part of the process.

4. When engaging an architect, make sure you understand the various phases that will be necessary to complete your project. It is important to understand how the project deliverables will build in detail, depth, and breadth of information.

5. How many drawings do you need? Does your project require a lean or comprehensive set of documents? This is a foundational question for your project and its team. If a lean project is desired, you may need a mechanism in place to create the additional information and details not included in the architect's drawing set during construction or rely heavily on your general contractor to make final decisions.

6. Bear in mind the amount of work that is required to complete three-dimensional renders for presentations. It may be quicker and more cost-effective to use two-dimensional drawings, material palettes, and precedent imagery.

7. Interior design has a lot of overlap with architecture. Make this scope part of early conversations with the architect to figure out the

options available. Make sure you understand the basic difference between an architect's and an interior designer's fee too.

8. FFE has many paths forwards. An in-depth conversation with the architect at the beginning of the project to understand these options will allow you to process and select the best one.

5
Working With Your Engineers

Engineers are specialists that work hand in hand with architects to complete aspects of your project design. There are various kinds of engineers. They typically fall into categories: mechanical, electrical, and plumbing (MEP) engineers and structural engineers, civil and geotechnical engineers, specialty engineers, etc. Specialist engineers could address any number of very specific circumstances or concerns for your specific project, from soil and geotechnical engineers to acoustic engineers. The project, depending on its depth and breadth, will require a specific balance of engineers to join the team. This should be discussed and determined as early as possible in the process to avoid unexpected timeline shifts and costs.

Your architect should obtain proposals and then make recommendations as to who they think should join the team. This is an aspect of the project where special attention should be paid to the schedule. It is desirable to align design professionals' scopes as much as possible. There are always many layers occurring simultaneously on your project and it's important to understand when everything is happening to make sure engineers are available to complete their tasks. It is easy to slow a project down here by not understanding how the various disciplines best slot together to achieve your overall deadline.

The various engineers are technically working for you on the project, but this can quickly become overwhelming, especially if you are not technically minded. To help, architects typically act as a prime consultant. This means all information for the design, drawings, specs, details, finishes, fixtures, and equipment ought to flow through them first. You can, should you wish, make this official with a Primary Consultancy Agreement with your architect. In this option, the architect holds all the engineers' agreements and manages their scopes and schedules. Many architects prefer to work this way as they often have long-standing relationships with engineers and other design professionals. One overall contract can speed up the process and make the working relationships between team members operate much more smoothly. It is more direct and flattens out the communication and coordination without needing additional effort from you. It is general industry practice that if you choose to operate in this way, your architect will treat their consultant fees as a reimbursable expense. This means that the architect will include the engineer's costs plus a markup on their invoice to you. The alternative to this scenario is for you to contract directly with each consultant and manage their outputs directly.

The engineering needs will vary a great deal based on your building type, location, and design. It is important to strategize as to which roles will be required to make up your project's engineering team at the beginning of the project with your architect. There are always options – a lean, inexpensive team is always possible, but the right team is ultimately best.

All the engineering work that goes into your project needs to be coordinated with the architectural design. Structural, mechanical, electrical, plumbing, and other disciplines will take up space between floors, ceilings, roofs, behind walls, and in cabinets throughout your finished building. The more integrated with the overall design they are, the more chance there is of ensuring they disappear. Unless intentional, your building's systems are best left out of sight. They should work in concert, but hidden away. A sign of a well-conceived, designed, and executed project is a lack of awareness of structural, mechanical, electrical, and plumbing systems in the finished building – unless intentional. Such systems should operate smoothly, without any thought at all from those living or working in the project.

Determining the engineering scope (or scopes) of work as part of the project's early phases will result in the best possible outcome.

Structural engineers

A structural engineer designs and determines the structural systems necessary for your project. The structural engineer will design the structural system for your project: the beams, columns, joists/rafters, floors, roofs, foundations, footings, and so on. They are the experts who can ensure the design stands up to the stresses and forces your building will be exposed to. Simply, they keep it standing. Some projects may not require a structural engineer. There are standard features that your architect may be able to handle. Depending on your requirements, having a structural engineer on the team, even on an hourly consulting basis can, however, add tremendous value. A structural engineer sees the project from a different perspective than the rest of the team, which means a new set of eyes. This means someone with a fresh take that can add professional experience to a situation and suggest appropriate and potentially time and cost-saving solutions. Whenever modifying existing buildings or building new structures, therefore, it is highly recommended to consider involving structural engineers.

WORKING WITH YOUR ENGINEERS

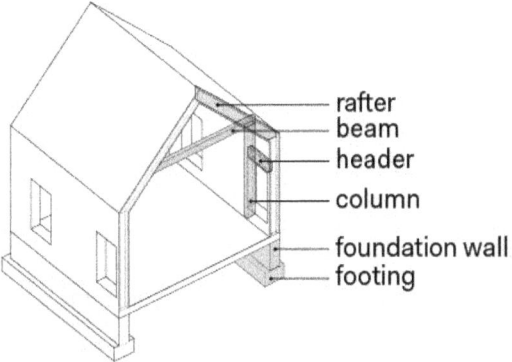

Basic beams, columns, rafters, headers, foundation wall, footings

Structural engineers perform as an integral part of the project team. It is reassuring to have them on the team. They help make the projects better, safer, and stronger.

Soil testing and geotechnical engineers

When embarking on a new building project, your architect will often begin by working with a structural engineer as their consultant to design the foundations as part of the wider structural system of your building. The foundation, however, relies on the actual strength of the earth in that exact location because it sits in the ground. That strength will vary depending on the exact place on the site. The strength of the ground is very important for the structural engineer. It can be difficult to design the foundations without this information.

A geotechnical engineer and their crew will typically come to the site with a boring machine on the back of a truck, drill holes to varying depths as specified by the structural engineer, take samples, and send them off to a laboratory for analysis.

The laboratory sends the analysis results to the geotechnical engineer who will interpret them and send a report to the structural engineer to feed into the foundation design. The detail will vary depending on the type of project, but armed with the soil analysis, the structural engineer will understand the forces and loads that the foundations will need to resist to keep it standing. As part of the building permit process, your local AHJ may want to see the soil report along with the structural design and calculations.

Other tests that can be performed on the soil will tell how well it will drain, which could impact the design of the foundation, waterproofing, and drainage systems. It could also tell what type of soil exists at different levels underneath the ground. Construction aside, these are all valuable pieces of information to have during the ownership of any real estate.

Soil testing does not need to cost a great deal for the value that is produced in preventative information measured against problems that might be costly to fix after the project is complete. An example of these problems might be differential settlement, which could cause structural cracks or a leaking foundation.

Both of these are very expensive and difficult to repair after the building is complete.

Mechanical (HVAC) engineers

Although mechanical engineering and heating, ventilation, and air conditioning are separate scopes of work, they often go together. These are considerable pieces of work and investment for your project and should be prioritized. They will each have different, but complementary, impacts.

Heating, ventilation, and air conditioning designs provide the active thermal comfort experienced on your project. This is the heating and cooling felt from your furnace, air conditioning, radiant floor system, or even a fireplace. To help, have conversations with your architect about what this means to the project early in the definition process. There are a wide variety of products and solutions available to keep your project comfortable. Cost is a real factor, but where you live and your lifestyle should certainly drive the decisions here.

Your building envelope design should be coupled with its mechanical systems, meaning your exterior walls, windows, and doors, etc, should be designed with the mechanical system in mind, and vice versa. This is an example of coordination. Having a thermal envelope that works in concert with your mechanical systems will provide the best and longest-lasting solution. Uncomfortable interior spaces and problems occur when these factors are out of balance, were not designed together, or were not adequately coordinated.

Mechanical engineers or designers, even working on a single-family home, ensure that the project uses the most appropriate equipment available. Having a specialist on board to design and verify that the relationship between equipment and envelope is in sync will result in a better outcome. Your architect will often design the envelope: exterior cladding, structural wall materials, insulation, air and vapor barriers, interior gypsum wall boards, windows, doors, skylights, and so on. They can also lead the placement of the mechanical systems, ductwork, and chases. The mechanical engineer or designer will follow and work with these parameters, providing feedback and coordinating their scope along the way. The architect will then make updates or changes to align the architecture with the mechanical system.

The mechanical system can take up a considerable amount of space behind walls and between floors in your project. This can be much more than the electrical or plumbing systems. When discussing your lifestyle, the most important parts of your home ought to be more than functional and practical. They should provide an experience where your thermal comfort is delivered by mechanical systems working silently in the background and with very little maintenance.

ARCHITECT'S ANECDOTE:
The value of mechanical engineers

We worked with a client whose home mechanical systems had been poorly engineered for the project and were too loud. 'They sound like a jet engine,' the client would exclaim. Their townhome was only six years old. It had been built as part of a much larger high-rise development made from a cast-in-place concrete wall-and-floor construction, with metal stud interior walls and a glass curtain wall system on the exterior. It was more akin to a commercial construction than a traditional residential framed home. I mention this because it's an important illustration of going into a project and providing a different perspective to the client.

When you are revising a mechanical system for noise, it is important to first check both the furnace unit itself and its location. The second consideration is the design and layout of the duct-runs throughout the home. This home had two existing forced-air furnaces, both of which were plagued by short return air duct and grill problems. The original mechanical engineers hadn't taken the commercial concrete construction into account, and did not want to coordinate the concrete construction with the appropriate duct-runs. Traditional, inexpensive systems had not been the best choice for this project from the start. What is more, replacing the ducts required the removal and replacement of 90% of the home interior walls and framing.

The finished system provided a nearly silent home living experience, which was a great outcome. A lot of this work, however, could have been avoided through appropriate mechanical engineering during the original design phase.

Electrical engineers

Typically, electrical engineering brings the power from the electrical grid into your project. Today, it may also include the installation of generators, solar panels, battery systems, and possibly wind turbines. This is vital, as there is so much in modern buildings that requires electricity. The current trend is moving away from natural gas towards electricity for heating, cooling, and cooking, and powering all of your building's equipment. If your project is a renovation or upgrade, you will probably already have a service to your property. A service might have to be run for a new-build construction.

The electrical system will need to be sized for the load that it will draw. This calculation is based on how many circuits, appliances, and features you will have in the building. Once this service is sized (including some spare capacity for the future), it cannot easily be changed. An electrician will install everything except the actual meter piece and the final connection to the neighborhood supply of power. Your architect, general contractor, and electrical engineer can steer the project where it needs to go for the electrical system to work. Your task is to make sure that you've thought of everything that will require electricity in your home.

Plumbing engineers (water and sewer)

With plumbing, the task is getting hot and cold water to your fixtures and managing how the wastewater leaves the building. When you're in an area with city water and sewer systems, your building is connected to these. If your site is more rural or remote, then you may need to consider digging a well for water and having a stand-alone septic system for the wastewater.

From an architectural and design perspective, the initial plumbing tasks center on defining locations and selecting fixtures for all cooking, washing, bathing, cleaning, and toilet spaces. It is important to select fixtures and equipment that work for you, your family, your lifestyle, and your tastes. When selecting plumbing fixtures with the architect, they will be thinking about coordinating all the elements in the property affected. This includes space inside walls and ceilings to run pipes, millwork, and tiling. Each selection needs to work together without conflict.

Once you get into the detail, the task is running pipes that will handle the flow of water in and out of your building. Fortunately, this follows old and simple principles of physics. However, there are many efficient and elegant solutions available that will ensure everything runs smoothly and components last longer. For example, locating as much of the plumbing system as possible in the same location by stacking elements can create greater efficiencies. Every bathroom, for instance, has a supply of hot and cold water. The cold water comes directly from either the city waterline or a local well. The hot water comes from your water heating source (water heater, tankless heater, or boiler). If your bathrooms are back to back, then they can share these lines. You will use less material and less water by volume in the system. This all equals less waste and lower energy requirements. The waste pipe from a scenario like this can also be combined, with these two bathrooms both feeding into a single drain. For the wastewater to exit or discharge from a building through gravity, air must be able to escape, so drains at the top will need to rise through the roof. A house with four bedrooms and four or five bathrooms could easily have five separate waste and vent stacks and five sets of supply lines. If the bathrooms are back to back and stacked, it might only need one or two. This efficiency will considerably reduce the material costs and labor required to build the system. Fewer pipes in general will expand the lifespan of the building by reducing maintenance requirements. The architect can explain the impact of plumbing decisions as part of the project definition phase, with a plumbing engineer joining the team to work out the details.

Overall, the engineering aspects of your project will have a major impact on how your property feels to live and work in. They ought to be given the right level of attention during the design phases, as fixing issues during or after construction can prove costly.

Practical thoughts on engineers

1. Depending on the scope of your project, you may need a structural engineer. This is typical for new construction. Have a conversation with your architect about their approach to this. Your architect should have a good relationship with a structural engineer. They can work with them behind the scenes in a seamless way to produce a well-coordinated workflow.

2. A soil or geotechnical engineer will only be necessary if you are building new foundations. This consultant will create a report that your structural engineer will use for their work. An early conversation with your architect about the cost and timing for this should happen. Make sure to obtain a copy of the soil report for your project records.

3. Mechanical design and engineering are very important. There is a wide spectrum of mechanical equipment available in the market today. Having a design consultant that can assist

with this scope will produce the best results and deliver a warm and comfortable home.

4. Electrical engineering depends on an accurate understanding of load. It's important to have a conversation with your architect about power use.

5. With a bit of thought, plumbing provides many opportunities to manage hot, cold, and waste water efficiently and save you time and money.

PART THREE
BUILDING YOUR PROJECT

This is the fun part! With your design documents in hand, the team has been assembled and is ready to realize the project's vision. It is time to put the shovels in the ground. This is where the architect passes the baton to the general contractor, and they begin to turn your dream into reality. Your contractor should kick off the process with a schedule, and then regular meetings between the owner (you), architect, and contractor. Such meetings are often referred to as OAC meetings and they are the ideal way to update everyone on progress.

You can't quite start straight away, though. You first need the go-ahead from relevant authorities.

6
Getting Permission To Build

A building permit is permission to build the project according to the contract documents submitted to the local Authority Having Jurisdiction (AHJ) for the project. Once approved, permits are required to be displayed on site for inspectors and the wider community during the construction process. Your permit will have a number or identification that will be linked to the records on file with the building department. It is also a record that is often searchable by address or number at your AHJ offices or online.

At the onset of a project, architects get passionate about design, details, materials, and experiences that will be enjoyed in the final product, but this is just one part of the project. There is also liaising with your local AHJ or building department. This involves encountering new processes, requests, and protocols, and can be a sobering and numbing experience to work through. There is little logic involved. It's like a standardized test, but one can become good at getting a permit approved by understanding the building codes and respecting the rules. Extraordinary design that does new things, however, is always a dance between the building codes and the project goals and objectives. The arbiter in this process is the AHJ, who often sees in black-and-white. In reality, the world of building codes exists in shades of gray.

This part of the process is where a lot of project energy can be used. It's advantageous for your architect to either have experience in the jurisdiction where your project is, or at the very least, do enough research to understand and get ahead of any items that could present pushback for the project. This could be as simple as having the correct building permit forms completed in the way the AHJ likes them. It could be as complex as understanding a certain code clause's interpretation by a specific AHJ and how the project will need to be adjusted to meet this. The AHJ will have a zoning and building department, as well as ancillary departments like historical preservation, environmental quality, water management, and others.

On the other side of these groups are the inspectors, who may or may not be in alignment with the building permit plans examiner. A building inspector can require a change on site that the building department

GETTING PERMISSION TO BUILD

did not require during the plans' examination. Inspections can happen during and after the work has been completed, and any changes they require typically come with a cost implication. A contingency in the budget can be helpful when this occurs. Your contractor must get approval from the inspectors during specific milestones throughout the construction process to keep building. There are times when the architect and engineers may need to meet with inspectors during construction to clarify and resolve an issue – occasionally involving the original plans examiner from the AHJ. This can require the design professionals to update or add drawings to be reviewed and approved again. These are all unexpected, time-consuming events that can typically be resolved quickly, but do impact the schedule, and occasionally require deviating from the desired design.

Building permits cost money and they are becoming increasingly more expensive. They are a client soft cost that should be accounted for with your other project professional fees. Building permits can also expire in one to one-and-a-half years. They can usually be renewed for this reason, but at an additional cost, so they ought to be arranged at the right time. Permits vary in use and scope. They can be received for simple repair and replacement work that might not require architectural drawings, such as the replacement of a kitchen in roughly the same layout that includes items such as new flooring, cabinets, countertops, appliances, and lights. Despite not needing drawings, this may require the homeowner to complete an application and pay a fee to the building department to receive a permit. AHJ websites are difficult at best to navigate. Most of the time, it's easier to call their office and speak to someone about what you are trying to achieve and how best to get there.

The challenge of obtaining building permits is an important conversation as you meet with architects at the beginning of your process. They should be able to give you local insight and talk you through available options. As a rough guide, simple no-drawing permits in a city jurisdiction such as Chicago, for example, may be received the same day, while it could take one to sixteen weeks for an expedited permit, or six to eighteen months for a traditional plan review permit. All these paths have a different effect on your project, its cost, opportunity costs, planning, and scheduling. Intimate knowledge of the nuances is very helpful to plan accordingly.

Another aspect of the typical AHJ of today worth discussing is communication. Somewhere along the evolution of the design and construction industry, AHJs have shifted their processes online. In this way, the communication methods have become 'inbound only' operations. Architects send all the project information to them, and if the design team, general contractor, or even you as the client, have questions, it may be next to impossible to receive answers. The AHJ simply provides comments on the drawings and documents that have been submitted. They can also ask for corrections. They are not generally available for discussion, so the permitting process can be a very frustrating phase. It is an advantage to have an experienced architect and design team working with you to acquire the correct paperwork and approvals.

Working with a permit expediter

Permit expediters are experts in the permit application process and can be very helpful. They typically act as the client's representative and acquire the permit on their behalf. One of the primary benefits of engaging an expediter is for their relationships with the AHJ. These relationships should increase the ability to coordinate with the reviewers. They are often very affordable too. Services, however, can be different from jurisdiction to jurisdiction and their value depends on your project size, complexity, and location. Permit expediters are more common in larger cities. For example, in a smaller Michigan jurisdiction, a building permit could be obtained with architectural drawings for an entire new building in less than a week. In a larger city like Chicago, it could take six to eighteen months for a permit on a similar-sized project.

It might benefit the project process to have a dedicated individual focusing on working with the building department. Time and cost savings are possible through working with someone who knows the ever-changing nuances of the application process and the staff at the building department. This may sound unbelievable, but experienced architects know what can happen once you send your project and application into a building department for review and it seems to become a moving target. Larger jurisdictions are more complicated and they have a large variety of personalities involved with the review of applications. There can also be opacity during the process and very little human interaction. In our digital and litigious age, especially when people in mid-level civic government roles are being asked to review architectural and engineering projects from a life and safety building code perspective, a culture of unresponsiveness has emerged and continues to exist.

The building permit process is an area where AI could be of tremendous value in the future. If there was a way to automate the review of projects by combining historical project review data cross-referenced with the various applicable codes and ordinances, it would revolutionize this part of the industry. Until then, architectural projects operate in a world of gray, manually navigating through the codes, ordinances, and rules.

If you choose to hire a permit expeditor, they take the project reins once the permit drawings and documents are complete. The expeditor could have little to no interaction with the architect. It may be advantageous to have more interaction with your architect, a kick-off page-turn meeting where the architect walks the expeditor through the project and spends time on unique project aspects. Then, if the expeditor is speaking to the building officials on behalf of the project, they will have a deeper understanding of the project and be better prepared to explain, defend, and answer questions when clarifying your intent and objectives. If the expeditor is not embedded into the project, they can often become an administrative extension of the building department policing the codes and ordinances instead of acting on your behalf. Early engagement with your architect is a subtle, and very important, opportunity to fold the expeditor into the project team in only a few meetings.

Your local Authority Having Jurisdiction (AHJ)

Most of the time, your AHJ will be your local zoning and building department. This may also include other government agencies overseeing the issuance of permits and inspections of construction or capital projects.

Zoning administers local land use ordinances. It covers your project and its surroundings, your land, site, or lot in the context of your neighborhood. Zoning ordinances must be followed covering set back (how far you are from the street), building height, floor-area-ratio (FAR), density, lot coverage, use and occupancy, and many more factors. The zoning department will often be adjacent to the building department – not specifically connected, but more complementary. Zoning is often the first step in the building permit process as it is required before beginning the building permit review process.

The building department enforces the local building codes and is responsible for issuing your building permit and inspecting the project throughout construction. Traditionally this department is composed of professional individuals, architects, and engineers that oversee or specialize in various disciplines such as mechanical, electrical, plumbing, and structural engineering. Once your project is submitted for permit review, these disciplines will take time to review the project and either approve it or provide comments and require corrections in accordance with their individual or collective understanding and interpretation of the building codes. In some cases, these officials make opinions while not understanding the project fully. It is the architect's or permit expediter's role to ensure building permit officials understand these project objectives and code interpretations. If there are still code compliance issues, then the architect will be required to make corrections before a building permit issuance.

Every jurisdiction uses different building codes. The US is migrating slowly to the International Building Code (IBC) and its versions. It would be remiss, here, not to explain that new codes come out approximately every two years. Jurisdictions choose which code and which year to adopt. It becomes immediately evident how complicated this becomes for the architects, engineers, and contractors. Some jurisdictions continue to use their own individual codes and seem unwilling to standardize.

All this means it is advantageous to work with a design professional that has experience with the local codes before your project or, if not, they ought to have a clear plan to overcome these hurdles. Experience tells us that there are always hurdles, and working in a jurisdiction for the first time can be difficult and time-consuming. Architects and engineers become local experts on how to assemble the most appropriate drawing and permit package for the building department, which is a subtle, yet powerful, advantage. For larger projects, there can be a design architect as well as the local architect specifically for this purpose. In this case, the local architect becomes the AHJ expert and becomes responsible for the permit document development and submission.

Building codes and your permit

Architects and engineers will design your project to comply with the building codes and ordinances that are enforced in your project's jurisdiction. It is important to remember these rules and regulations are in place for the safety and wellbeing of the people in the community. Real-world examples include requiring smoke and carbon monoxide detectors in each bedroom, ensuring office entrance doors are 36in wide, or making sure that wheelchairs can move freely throughout a building. Building codes are necessary; however, their many clauses can have different interpretations. The building permit process works best if the AHJ has a process to talk through the interpretive nature of the various codes. Pre-internet, most jurisdictions accepted paper drawings for building permit review. This review was an in-person process that allowed conversations and meetings to clarify the design team's work and their interpretation of the various codes. Many jurisdictions have now moved the permit intake process online, requiring digital drawings rather than paper. In doing so, they have removed the in-person, human interaction. This is great for many reasons, including increasing the speed of review, allowing review by various disciplines simultaneously, and reducing the amount of paper consumed in the process. It also allows the jurisdiction to decide how they want to communicate. (As we've discussed, this seems to be one way.) The digital permit intake process is still evolving and has a way to go to get back to the collaborative nature it once was.

When design professionals begin to work with a site or an existing building, the building code sets boundaries that need to apply to any situation. Every new design project is, of course, slightly different, and the more innovative a design solution is, the more likely it is to push these boundaries. In these cases, the code becomes the tool used to make sure that the building still complies with life and safety requirements. This needs to be demonstrated ahead of the client's goals and objectives. This means a careful balancing act is required between the building department, inspectors, the project drawings and specifications, and, importantly, how your general contractor and other subcontractors interpret these instructions. There are a lot of moving parts to this process, and it's not typically done until the final inspections are complete and, ultimately, your new building is in use.

A building permit or permission to build is granted by the AHJ after they have approved an application. The application submission is project-specific and can vary depending on your goals and objectives. It is worth visiting the local AHJ's building department website to find which of the many different types of permits apply to your project. Many AHJs separate their permits into project types – simple repair and replacement, deck and porch building, interior remodeling, new buildings, and items like signage, landscaping, and others are all activities that can require permits. The premise of obtaining a permit is to ensure compliance with the codes and ordinances, approval of the design, inspections throughout the construction process, and then to verify compliance at the end. In some cases, ongoing or yearly inspections may be necessary depending on the type of permit, occupancy, or building. As the building owner, you are often technically the permit applicant, so you are ultimately responsible for what happens on the project and property. The architect, general contractor, client representative, or a combination of players may be managing the permit and inspection process to a greater or lesser extent, but it remains your project and responsibility. The final decisions are yours and everyone ought to be acting under your direction. The architect, design team, and contractors are merely technical instruments creating drawings and documents and constructing according to the goals and objectives illustrated and explained in the contract documents.

ARCHITECT'S ANECDOTE:
An early AHJ experience

I was sixteen years old and working for my father's construction company part-time while in high school. One of his clients wanted to turn their existing basement garage into a guest suite and my father asked if I could create some architectural drawings for the project. Little did I know that the drawings I created on my drafting table by hand with pencil on paper would be presented to the city council for approval of a zoning variance to allow an existing garage to be converted to sleeping quarters. Well, it succeeded!

A lot of the principles in this book came to me at an early age. The secret is simply clearly defining what it is you are looking to do, presenting it to the right people, and working through the project until the desired solution is complete. There are obviously many steps along the way, and this may be one of the most expensive capital expenditures that you ever make, but remember: simple, hand-drawn plans did the job for a high school student.

You are not expected to navigate the specifics of building permits alone. Your design team and construction professionals will be better advocates for you, especially when the process feels opaque and is hard to understand. It is always a celebration when permits are issued. The moment should be enjoyed, and this milestone should not be taken for granted. It is a journey and a process, and it takes the entire team to make it happen.

The permit application process and costs

The permit process involves completing and submitting an application to the local AHJ for review and approval. Each AHJ has an individual application process, usually available for download. They are likely to want an application pack containing property information, a project description, and owner, architect, contractor, and subcontractor details. It will also ask for a value for the construction. This may be used in part to determine the cost of the permit. Any drawing requirements will relate specifically to your project. They won't necessarily need to see everything. The AHJ may only require a few drawings to approve and grant building permission.

Once the drawings and documents are reviewed, the architect and engineers may receive comments that require responses in the form of drawing and document corrections. In some cases, the reviewers give the design team 'boiler-plate' comments that are already addressed in the documents and drawings, and it turns into an exercise of showing the reviewers where to look. At other times, the reviewers have different interpretations of the codes and ordinances than the design professionals, which prompts a conversation to clarify which, if any, drawings require updating. Sometimes conversation is helpful, and other times it is not.

This is a 'behind the curtain' exercise in the project process that you may feel removed from – many times for good reasons. The building permit process can be a stressful and frustrating part of the project that remains opaque to everyone. Yet, building codes and ordinances are in place to protect the health, safety, and welfare of the community and it is essential to stay safely within the boundaries that the codes and ordinances set.

Permit costs, like everything else, seem to be rising. Each AHJ has a method of determining what these costs are using a formula of some sort. Your

AHJ should publish the permit costs and be able to produce individual methods when asked. For simple residential projects, the permit fees can be between $500–$10,000. More complicated residential and commercial projects can be higher. Fees are also often expressed as a percentage of the overall project value.

Local permit strategies

Achieving your permits can require some strategic thinking, especially if you sense your project will test the AHJ boundaries. Your architects can recommend different paths through this process depending on the circumstances of the project. This is a conversation to have early in the process with your architect, and possibly with the AHJ too, if possible.

To a certain degree, your strategy will be defined by your location. Large cities such as Chicago and New York, for example, have specific permits that are designed to speed up review and approval for certain project types. For instance, in Chicago, there is a self-certified permit route where architects with specific local qualifications can apply for expedited permits for projects that follow the right guidelines. This can mean a dramatic saving in permit time for your project. It is worth checking to see if there's an equivalent in your area.

Practical thoughts on permit or permission to build

1. Your building permit is the approval needed for you, the owner, to get started. This is a milestone for the project. With a permit in hand, you are permitted to begin construction. Celebrate!

2. Your local AHJ is the approving body. It is your responsibility to ensure the application is correct and that your project is, ultimately, delivered as permitted. The design professionals and contractors are working on your behalf.

3. Professional permit expediters can be very useful partners on your project. Speak to your architect early on in your process to determine the composition of your team and the best path to acquiring permission to build.

4. Building codes are very real, legal documents that your project is required to comply with to protect your community's wellbeing. Failure to follow the rules and regulations is a serious matter.

5. The permit process varies greatly between AHJs. Make sure you understand what is involved early in your project to ensure that expectations are accurate and appropriate planning can be made.

6. Poorly planned, understood, or executed permit applications waste time and money. Explore avenues to develop the right strategy for your project, including local expedited options if they exist.

7
Working With Your General Contractor

If it still feels like you are preparing to build, then you are right. There are still a few steps to take before construction can start. The next task is to establish your working relationship with the general contractor who will realize the design documents by actually undertaking the construction. The three most often used project delivery methods today are as follows:

1. Traditional design-bid-build
2. Design-preconstruction-build
3. Design-build

Design-bid-build

Traditional design-bid-build is a siloed approach. This is a model where you hire an architect to design and create drawings and documents for the building permit process and, ultimately, construction. Once these drawings and documents are complete, they are sent out to several general contractors who competitively bid for the work. This is sometimes also known as a tendering process. General contractors are tasked with responding to the proposed scope of work with a price based on their projected costs for labor and materials. Today, for a standard domestic project, it can take between two and six weeks for general contractors to provide bids for you to review, often in conjunction with the architect fielding questions, providing clarifications, and visiting the site. It is generally undertaken on the assumption the lowest bid will win the job.

With design-bid-build, general contractors are not paid for bidding time or, of course, guaranteed to win. The incentive to invest significant time on your project is low, which can yield inaccurate numbers and a poor understanding of the scope and project. At best, this method can be a way to control project costs but, overall, it is an opaque process that does not often yield the best results or necessarily create an efficient or effective project team.

Design-preconstruction-build

This is a hybrid approach that can take on various forms, but removes the element of competition on price. Good architects should have a good understanding of costs and work very hard to design wisely. This means your architect can collaborate with a chosen general contractor during a pre-construction phase early on in the design process of work to present you with a project price in partnership. Architects gain cost information earlier through this way of working. General contractors gain a deeper understanding of your project too. A design-preconstruction-build process better aligns the architect and general contractor with your project goals. This should produce a faster, better-quality project at a fairer cost. It makes a historically competitive and cost-driven process much more transparent and quality-focused. The decision point comes at the end of a joint pre-construction phase of activity. You still may not want to work with the general contractor proposed, but the likelihood of this happening is greatly reduced.

Design-build

This model is where your architect is, or acts, as your general contractor. There are many variations of this model. Indeed, the term 'design-build' feels stretched out of any useful definition. General contractors that enjoy relationships with designers or architects often offer design-build services or call themselves design-builders without really embracing it as a methodology. A true design-build process is one delivered under a single prime consultant that connects the design and building process under one umbrella. It is a single effort for your project that can result in a very strong project when executed well. Design-build is often contractor-led, but can also be architect-led. Be sure to understand the difference and choose the path that best suits you and your needs.

If you are interested in a design-build approach, the interviewing process should be thorough. It is essential to see examples and understand the infrastructure that the company has. Meet the people and hear how they approach combining these services. Speak to people they have worked with. This is the combination of two separate skill sets (architecture and construction) into a single entity. You need to trust that entity a great deal.

ARCHITECT'S ANECDOTE:
Selection in action

A very good general contractor we work with referred us to a client who was acquiring a family home that they wanted to completely gut, start over, with an addition. We were excited to be included and happy to be collaborating with a contractor that we knew and trusted.

We sent the client our proposal and interviewed for the project with success. We were awarded the project and began work. Our process was to fully document the building by measuring it, creating existing conditions drawings on site by hand, and taking extensive photographs. These were then used to create the digital architectural model that would become the design and drawings for the project.

By the end of the process, the client seemed happy and understood the plans and renderings we presented, which included accurate finishes, fixtures, and equipment, as well as suggestions on furniture. Once the project began construction, however, the client chose not to include us for contract administration work. Their contractor reinforced this idea because they were a developer-contractor, so they preferred to make the decisions on design, finishes, and fixtures directly with the client themselves.

We were left trying to figure out if the client had misunderstood our presentations, or if they disliked what was presented and specified. The fact remains that there was a disconnect between our process, what was presented, and what the client took away. From our perspective, the final project result was inferior to what we designed, because compromises had been made by the contractor without our input.

Understanding the general contractor's role

It is important to understand the difference between your relationship with the architect and the general contractor. The architect is a design professional and a professional business. Like a doctor, lawyer, or accountant, your architect is licensed and bound by state statutes or similar regulations. You pay for their time and expertise. Your contractor is, first and foremost, a business that builds tangible, physical things for profit. General contractors are licensed and regulated too, but this relates to the business rather than the individual. With a general contractor, you are paying for materials and labor. They are two very different modes of operation. Your architect is most likely to be a designer first and a businessperson second. It is important you share a vision and align your goals. Your general contractor is a businessperson first, who is primarily tasked with getting the work done. As illustrated in the diagram below, you have a direct contractual relationship with both your architect and your general contractor, and your architect and general contractor have an indirect contractual relationship with each other through you.

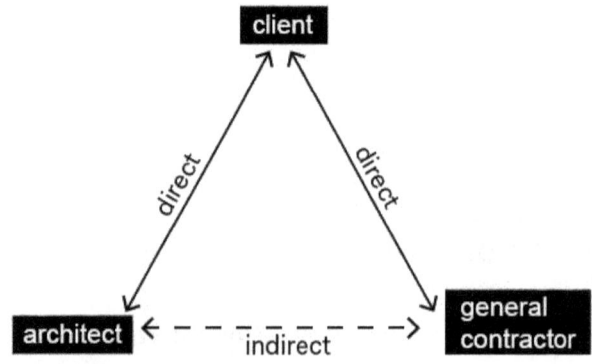

Primary client relationships

The most important factor in selecting a general contractor is 'fit'. Fit depends on the project goals and objectives, the amount of capital available to invest in the project, and the schedule. The schedule and investment are relatively straightforward to check. Can the general contractor complete the work on time and within the available budget? Your goals and objectives are less black-and-white, but will drive the results, detail, and level of finish your project requires. This, in turn, gives you the characteristics you need from your general contractor. These factors may feel complicated, but, assuming you haven't gone for a design-build contract, a strong architect can assist you with the process of research, shortlisting, interviewing, comparing, and then selecting your general contractor. When the architect has experience with your project type and in your market, they should come to the project with the appropriate contractors in mind. Finding the right fit is important because, ultimately, your project can only be as good as your general contractor. Every contractor has experience, strengths, and weaknesses. Success comes through carefully matching these with your project objectives.

It is worth reiterating the value of the design-pre-construction-build model here. Working with *one* contractor from an early phase of the project and involving them in design and planning meetings can yield much higher results than a selection process based on competitive bidding. Paying a general contractor for their time upfront in the project will generally save you money in the long run too.

However you go about the selection process, your architect should have a formal and transparent approach to meeting potential contractors. This should involve a face-to-face meeting. If you are working with an existing site and building, the initial meeting should be on site with the architect looking at a set of preliminary design documents. This will yield the most meaningful introduction to the project and the individuals involved. Ideally, this meeting should end with the general contractor having enough information and schematic drawings to begin pricing.

Scheduling multiple contractor meetings can be time-consuming, but they are worth planning carefully. It is best not to overlap them too closely as it's always awkward for one contractor to see the next on the way in or out. The world of architecture, design, and construction is no doubt smaller than you would imagine in your location. The chances of people recognizing each other is high. Understanding your competition is one thing, but having some mystery in this process can go a long way.

ARCHITECT'S ANECDOTE:
The value of relationships over cost

We were introduced to a new client by a general contractor we respected and really liked to work with. They had previously executed our work flawlessly, so we were excited that this new project was happening. We took the client through a quick, fun, and productive design process that achieved great results and most of the client's dreams were realized in the design of the new home.

Once our initial design work was complete, we suggested sending the project over to the general contractor for pricing to begin defining a budget. The client felt the general contractor's costs were higher than what they wanted to spend. This created a series of intense meetings to figure out where savings might be possible, but the general contractor stood firm on their numbers and the client was uncompromising on their wants. This led the client to seek another contractor to price the project for comparison. We did not know the other general contractor, but some research indicated that they were not at the same level as our recommended general contractor, and we communicated our thoughts to the client.

The new general contractor was also a developer, which meant a different approach and perceived lower fees. Based on saving money, our client chose to ignore previous relationships which, for us, felt like a missed opportunity. Experience has taught us that working with people that understand you and that you have a relationship with means more than numbers on a quote. When the numbers are not aligning with expectations, the remedy is the right conversation, not necessarily finding someone new who may quote the way you want them to.

When this project was complete, we were convinced that the client had spent more with the developer general contractor than they had expected and achieved an inferior result. This could all be attributed to communication during the early phases of the project and what we perceive was a lack of understanding of the budgeting process.

Signing a general contractor's agreement

You've selected a general contractor. How do you now hold them accountable to deliver your project? Typically, general contractors have their own standard agreements. They will often recommend that these be used to save time and legal wrangling. However, it should not be surprising to find these agreements are probably written to favor the general contractors' interests. Therefore, it's recommended that you at least explore alternatives before signing anything, or as an alternative, have your attorney thoroughly review the agreement.

The American Institute of Architects (AIA) has standard contracts that are available for use and can be purchased at minimal costs. The AIA, given its industry role, knows the design and construction process intimately. It spends considerable time and effort maintaining its contracts as best practice documents and vets case law to make sure that, legally, everything remains current. It should also be noted that AIA contracts are designed to be a starting point. It is always good to consult qualified legal professionals to work through customizing clauses and, if required, negotiate around the specific requirements for your project.

While most contractual arrangements run smoothly, involving an attorney in signing an agreement can also provide benefits should something go wrong. In the case of a dispute, independent advice from a legal expert already familiar with the relationship between you and your contractor can be very helpful.

Lien waivers should form part of any agreement with a general contractor. The term 'lien' refers to the right of a supplier to withhold a customer's property as recourse in the case of non-payment. A lien waiver is a legal mechanism through which your general contractor acknowledges payments and, accordingly, renounces any lien rights. Partial lien waivers should be collected at each project payment milestone. The same applies to anyone the general contractor hires on a subcontractor basis. A lien waiver from your roofing contractor, for example, ought to clarify that non-payment by the general contractor is an issue for them. If you have the correct lien waivers, you are protected from spurious liabilities.

There are occasions when the general contractor does not pay their subcontractors even though you have settled their bill. This is a red flag and an indication that larger problems exist within the project. The most important thing to note is your role should not include mediating in these circumstances. The best protection that you can have is a signed lien waiver that proves you have settled your bills and there is no recourse available for anyone to collect funds from you. The process can feel an administrative burden, especially for small businesses, but lien waivers are an important part of the agreement with your general contractor and their subcontractors that ought not to be overlooked.

Working with subcontractors

Subcontractors are the trades that your general contractor will hire to help them complete your project. The list of trades depends on your project, but will typically include mechanical installers, electricians, plumbers, carpenters or framers, finish carpenters, drywallers, insulators, flooring installers, concrete subs, excavators, roofers, welders, steel fabricators, millworkers, and landscapers, etc. It will also include all the vendors that will supply the materials, equipment, finishes, fixtures, and so on to the general contractor and their subs to install. There could be more than a hundred people working on your project. Any complete organizational chart of your project is likely to resemble an extensive family tree. The general contractor's primary role is to organize and manage all these different people, groups, and companies in keeping the project on track and at the costs agreed to. This is a daunting task from the outside, even if the project is running smoothly. This is why it is essential to feel comfortable with your chosen general contractor's capabilities.

The subcontractors ought to be kept at arm's length from you by the general contractor. They act as your primary point of contact, and all project construction communication (including subcontractor correspondence) should be routed through them. The general contractor may send questions or requests from their subcontractors directly to the architect and engineers, who accept, log, and respond to these on your behalf. In this way, your architect will use their expertise to guide the project. It is natural to feel a little left out as the client, but the old adage that 'no news is good news' applies here. A lack of communication can be a sign that all is going well.

This is because it is the general contractor's role to ensure the level of subcontractor skill and experience matches the level, type, complexity, and sophistication of the project. An appropriate general contractor should have relationships with multiple subcontractors. They will also always have favorites. If the project has elements that are particularly complicated, custom, or of special importance, it can be useful for a general contractor to work with a proven subcontractor they are familiar with. Equally, they should have a broad range of subcontractors on hand to ensure they can be flexible and responsive.

Without getting involved in the details, you should be comfortable with your general contractor's approach to subcontractor relationships.

ARCHITECT'S ANECDOTE:
The value of subcontractor expertise

We had a client who wanted to renovate their home because their heating system wasn't efficient. Even though it was a small project, as the architects, we felt we needed a specialist to fully investigate and design an efficient, high-performing, and, most importantly, cost-effective system. We knew what the project needed, and engaging a mechanical engineer was the right path.

We had discussed the issue with the general contractor, and they confirmed they had a relationship with a suitably qualified mechanical subcontractor who could help build the designed system. We didn't concern the client with the details, and their relationship with us and the general contractor wasn't affected. The mechanical subcontractor did a great job, including last-minute changes during the close-out of the project to save even more in operating costs.

This is one of the most successful mechanical systems we've delivered on a residential project. With an expert on the team, we pushed the boundaries of technology to achieve excellent results. The client experienced uninterrupted service without the need for any input and was delighted.

Starting the construction process

Only when you are comfortable with your general contractor and have an agreement that seems equitable to all sides, can construction begin. The general contractor and their subcontractors, armed with the project's building permits and architect's drawings and documents, can mobilize. This is always an incredibly exciting phase to watch. While experiencing construction taking shape and turning ideas that were discussed on paper into reality is a thrill for you and your architect, it is very much business as usual for the general contractor. This can lead to a slight sense of anti-climax, but in a well-planned project, there is very little for you, as the client, to contribute.

Owner, architect, and contractor (OAC) meetings should be held on site regularly. This will ensure you see the process from start to finish and gain a deeper understanding of, and connection to, your project. It can be a life-changing experience to be involved in construction, which should be celebrated. Your general contractor will, however, want to get on with the job.

Detailed schedule

The schedule is probably the most important aspect of the project at this stage. Creating and maintaining the schedule is an administrative task for the general contractor. They should be held responsible for any slippage. Smaller general contractors may try to avoid schedules, and this should always be a red flag. These companies can find it difficult to create and maintain a schedule because there are so many moving parts to construction projects, including subcontractors that are constantly changing their work plans and availability. Smaller contractors often have a feast-or-famine relationship with their work. At times when they are quiet, they will dedicate themselves to your project. When they get busy, they'll juggle your project with others. This can mean running short of labor and materials, or even leaving your project for another altogether in an emergency situation. These are real-world situations, and why the general contractor is so important. They need to effectively manage this on your behalf. The schedule is the mechanism that makes this happen. The schedule:

- Forms the basis of communication on the project during every phase of construction.

- Is the document that you might need to share with your lender to mark off against financial milestones.

- Is how your architect identifies the ideal time for site visits to check work completion and quality.

- Is how completion and move-in are planned.

- Is the document that keeps everyone on track and accountable.

Seasons

Spring, summer, and fall are very important for construction. People do their best to take advantage of days when the weather allows easy work outside, for example. The winter months can add costs and time to your project. Many subcontractors will simply not want to work when it is too cold or wet. Temporary protection from the elements may be required to allow people to work efficiently and protect building materials. Many materials require dry conditions and specific temperatures for installation such as adhesives, glues, paints, sealants, membranes, concrete, masonry-based products, and more. These all have guidelines that must be followed for correct installation.

When first meeting with the architect, it is therefore wise to look at the current calendar. By looking at the design, permitting process, and pricing timeline, it is possible to anticipate a construction start date. This can be adjusted to maximize efficiency for your specific project scope and allow for seasonal weather in your location.

Contract administration

Contract administration is a task that goes on throughout the construction phase of the project. It is best to consider your arrangement with the architect and general contractor as a living document that needs keeping up to date. All projects change and evolve as they progress. Even the best-laid plans are occasionally faced with unexpected events and surprises. The key to successfully managing change in your project is remembering that the architect is your advocate on the project. Architects have valuable experience and project understanding at a higher level than contractors, who may be embedded in detail. Architects monitor your project through the lens of design. They can match details, materials, and finishes to the contract documents quickly and effectively. They are best placed to spot changes and suggest solutions to problems too. Because they authored your project drawings in the first place, your architect is in the prime position to be monitoring the building process and to be steering the general contractor as required.

ARCHITECT'S ANECDOTE:
The value of an architect on site

We were working on an interior project for a townhome in Chicago. During the lengthy and highly specific design process, we scoured the industry to find very specific porcelain tiles for the bathrooms. The bulk of them were in a dark gray with a lighter gray veining. The tiles were air-freighted from Spain due to a very constrained project schedule. On a weekly site visit, I noticed a pallet of tiles and suspected the colors had been reversed. Light gray outnumbered dark gray. After raising the question, the general contractor confirmed that this was, indeed, the case. The tiles were swapped with a new, immediate order and the general contractor was able to juggle various trades while the new tiles were en route so the schedule was preserved.

The point here is that I was able to spot the tile error because I had an understanding of the design that the general contractor did not. As the project was busy, it was likely that the wrong colors would have been installed which, at best, would have led to a grumpy client. At worst, it would have meant a lengthy process of removing and replacing the tiles at a more costly later stage. As it was, the mistake was rectified with minimal impact.

Contract administration is an activity that you may want to handle without the assistance of your architect. You may wonder if the architect's fee can be saved during construction. In making the decision, it is worth balancing the risks of mistakes being made and the additional costs and delays that might cause.

The architect, of course, also authored the project documents and created every drawing, detail, diagram, and table that the general contractor and their subcontractors use during construction. The architect should intimately know each decision that is in the drawing set and where to find every piece of information required to build your project. A comprehensive project can have as many as hundreds of drawing sheets that are 24" × 36" in size, or larger. If a technical question or contractual issue arises, imagine how long it might take the general contractor to find the answer and fully understand what they are supposed to build. This is a significant task that often works far more efficiently when the architect that authored the drawings is involved.

Inspections and punch lists

Let us assume that the project has run smoothly and is wrapping up and very near completion. Things can feel to happen quickly, especially as contractors and subcontractors have the prospect of final payments on the horizon. They are typically keen to complete their scope promptly, get paid, and then move on to their next jobs. However, there are a few hurdles to overcome before this can happen.

Final inspections will need to be coordinated with your local AHJ inspectors, who will need to confirm the construction is complete to code and matches the approved construction documents. You, of course, will need to be satisfied with the work too. Inevitably, there will be areas of dissatisfaction that need fixing before you're happy to consider the contract complete. In the construction industry, a list of final client concerns is often referred to as a 'punch list'. Involving your architect can reduce the extent of changes on this final step. Site visits as the project comes to a close can support wrapping up tasks amicably. If outstanding or missing scope can be completed while contractors are still on the project, for example, it is far easier and less expensive for them to complete tasks. Having to call back contractors who may have moved on to new work is always more challenging.

In some cases, tradespeople may not be aware of outstanding tasks. Through an understanding of contract documents and managing appropriate communication, you have a much better chance of a smooth completion. Indeed, a larger commercial, industrial, or institutional project may have a dedicated specialist completion consultant who handles the close-out process. This may be referred to as 'commissioning' the building. Commissioning is a term for the entire process, from closing the project out to testing all the building systems and operations, identifying how each piece of equipment is to be operated and maintained, and documenting items that do not conform to the contract and need to be corrected. For a house or a smaller project, a specialist may not be necessary, but it is still important to pay particular attention to the final weeks and days of a schedule. The fit and finish of the project must match the contract documents, and everything should work as expected, by you, before the contract can be considered delivered.

If you have a responsible project team and have engaged the architect to administer the contract throughout construction, the best measures will have been in place to avoid issues and ensure that your project is completed as intended. Ongoing observation during construction on your behalf from the creators of the design package is the best course of action. The agreement that you have with your general contractor requires that they build exactly what is in the design package. This is what you are paying for. Any deviations, discrepancies, or deficiencies are the responsibility of your contractor to correct and complete.

A warranty period should also be written into the contractor agreement. This means any deficiencies that arise during the first year after close-out, for example, are repaired by the contractor at their cost.

You may feel time pressure to move into your property and put the construction phase behind you. Close-out can also be stressful, which means opportunities to handle the situation well can be missed. It pays not to feel rushed. Besides, walking into a newly completed project for the first time is a great moment to experience. It is always very personal and moving. It can be life changing.

It can also take time to use new spaces, test all your new fixtures and appliances, and experience places at different times of the day and in different seasons. Architecture should challenge your perceptions of the project enough to allow surprise and wonderful moments long after the drama of construction has subsided.

Practical thoughts on contractors

1. Selecting your general contractor is very important. They must have experience with the same type of project you would like to complete, they need to be able to show their availability for your project, be excited to complete what has been designed, and respect your design professionals.

2. Subcontractors will be hired, managed, and paid for by your general contractor. Despite being managed at arm's length, make sure the subcontractors that your general contractor is hiring are capable and appropriate for the scope of your project.

3. Make sure that your general contractor has a track record of projects completed by the same subcontractors they are using for your project. It may also be wise to see and assess subcontractors separately.

4. Ensure the lien waiver contractual mechanism is clear and understood by your contractor and subcontractors. It is important to protect you financially, and shouldn't just be seen as an administrative burden.

5. The schedule is one of the most important administrative tools for your project. Verify that your general contractor will create, maintain, and follow a schedule as a live document.

6. Hold your general contractor accountable for the schedule and communicate it to allow planning for site visits, payments, and associated scope that relates to the construction of your project.

7. Contract administration is one of the most overlooked and important phases of your project. Everything rests on the general contractor's ability to fulfill the scope of work they've agreed to. Your architect is the best person to be an ongoing resource for these questions. Don't overlook this phase – especially not to save money.

8. Once final AHJ inspections have taken place, the punch list is your final opportunity to get deficiencies corrected. If you have your architect spearhead the close-out phase of the project, you can typically speed up the process and work towards fewer items that need fixing.

Epilogue

We've reached the end of the construction project. You have the keys of your new project. Minor fixes aside, you should be celebrating with your project team. Don't send them off to their next project quite yet.

There is the future to consider.

8
Living In Your Project

Questions about your project are very likely to arise in the weeks, months, if not years, that follow the excitement of completion. This is to be expected. If the project had regular OAC meetings during the construction process, the questions and deficiencies should be minimal, but construction is a complex process. You would be a highly unusual client if you understood it all and didn't have worries after you took the keys. It is important to agree on the next steps, because some architects prefer a 'hands-off' experience, moving quickly from one project to the next, while others are happy to stay involved in the life of their buildings after they are finished. All, however, should be able to adjust and adapt to your requirements. It is important that you discuss your preference prior to the end of the contract.

Having realistic expectations is important too. Perfection is extraordinarily difficult and magic wands to fix problems do not exist. Understanding that slight deficiencies with the general contractor's work is normal and including provisions in your contract for them is vital. Your architect can advise you on things to consider. It is worth running relevant clauses past your legal adviser too. A reputable general contractor should be happy to discuss the process of resolving any of your concerns.

There are 'nuts and bolts' aspects to every project. You will need to know how things work and which buttons to press, for example. Your general contractor ought to have manuals for each piece of equipment, appliance, and fixture they have worked hard to install. They should, as a minimum, ensure that all these manuals are passed on to you intact at the end of the project. It may be that they are organized into an easily accessible system for you. Depending on the complexity of your project, you may be invited to a commissioning meeting, or series of meetings. Commissioning refers to a formal handover where you, as the client, are taught how your finished project operates, including all the hardware, equipment, system, services, and fixtures. This may seem simple and straightforward – but it's not always, especially once you consider equipment warranties and maintenance requirements.

There are so many things that will need to be done preventatively to maintain your new property to ensure it has a long life. It is important you understand them, as well as any third-party suppliers you need to engage with. It is always prudent to use your contractor, their subcontractors, and your architect as a resource here. Acquire a contact sheet from them that includes the contact details of people and businesses who furnished and installed equipment so you are armed for future maintenance or repair.

ARCHITECT'S ANECDOTE:
The power of a contact list

Long after we had finished their project, one of our clients noticed new streetlights being installed on their neighborhood block. During the work, the installers reportedly crossed some wires and caused the primary neighborhood transformer to malfunction, sending double the prescribed voltage to all the buildings on the block. Our client happened to be home during the resulting surge and had the presence of mind to unplug equipment from the wall and shut off all the electrical breakers. However, some systems, including the property's furnace, condenser, boiler, fans, etc, were still affected.

While neighbors struggled to rectify problems, the client was able to contact the original electrical and mechanical subcontractors thanks to the information furnished by their general contractor. Things were fixed in the next few days as a result of a thorough commissioning manual and contact list.

On a large project, provision for the 'installer list' ought to be written directly into your general contractor agreement and should include all product and equipment manuals and warranty information. It is important that all product and equipment warranties are in your name and any confirmations are passed along to you. Some warranties depend on being registered by the owner and may not be honored otherwise. This is an easy step, but it is sometimes overlooked by smaller general contractors who may not have sufficient administrative resources. In these cases, what often takes place when there is a problem is that you call the general contractor with a sense of urgency, but they have moved on and aren't motivated to help. This is especially true after the typical one-year warranty period, and you may find yourself alone with the problem.

Pragmatic thoughts aside, you should love your project! It was created specifically for you, and is something that should be celebrated and enjoyed from the moment you move in.

9
Conclusion

There are many books in the world on the subject of architecture. Having written this one, I cannot claim originality to writing on architecture. Architecture has been written about since it has existed as a profession and there are great works of analysis and criticism by learned professionals. Whether your interest is in the real history of ancient buildings or imagined future cities, there are countless authors I could recommend. The canon, however, isn't full of actual, real-world, practical advice for clients. This was my goal with *Speaking Architecture*. If, as someone embarking on a construction project, you have picked up one or two practical pieces of advice, hints, or tips, then I will consider the book a success.

My intention in putting pen to paper wasn't necessarily to turn you into architects. The art and science of designing architecture is about finding harmony between material, space, light, and experience and, rightly, takes a long time and a lot of training to perfect. Rather than train readers, I wanted to empower them to make informed decisions about their construction projects that resonate with their individual needs and aspirations. I know, however, that as a client, you only have limited time. The insights presented within this book should feel relatively straightforward and, if not easy, then certainly immediately applicable.

Having reached the conclusion, if you feel more confident discussing your ideas with an architect than you did previously, then there is nothing more to add. I can probably leave you here. I wish you well with your project.

ARCHITECT'S ANECDOTE:
Good news

I wanted to finish the book with a note on success. In June 2020, the world was a challenging place. We were in the midst of the Covid pandemic, and the news was dominated by masks and shutdowns. We were beginning to understand that this was not necessarily a short-term situation, but no one really knew for sure.

Our practice was like every other business out there – some of our most important projects were put on hold and pending cancellation. It was a frightening time. Then the phone rang. A client wanted to build a new

CONCLUSION

house in Southwest Michigan, about an hour-and-a-half from our office in Chicago. We were, of course, very interested. But how could we meet? How could we learn about the client and their needs and wants? How could we understand the site? How could we work with our consultants and the jurisdiction? There were so many questions.

This client was just the best. They were young, but wise beyond their years. We learned to meet remotely. We learned about each other. We used our creative process. As an architectural practice, we were, fortunately, able to keep working together in the same space, masked and distanced for nearly the entire, intense period of Covid. On this project, we successfully took the client through the entire design process right into the pricing and permit phases without a single in-person meeting. It wasn't until we were about to break ground that we met our client face-to-face.

It is also worth mentioning that the AHJ was still able to accept and review the project in a timely manner. The general contractor was able to price and organize the beginning of the project without any special considerations. The project progressed in a manner that was not typical, yet it was very successful.

The resulting new family home took approximately fifteen months to construct. It began in the fall of 2020 and was ready in the new year of 2022. The client achieved their goals and enjoys the new place they call home.

I share this because it is a reminder that *Speaking Architecture*, even in the most trying of circumstances, can, and does, lead to success.

Glossary

AIA (American Institute of Architects)

The American Institute of Architects (AIA) is a professional organization for architects in the United States. It was founded in 1857 and currently has over 90,000 members. The AIA provides support and resources to architects to help them improve the quality of their work, advocate for the value of architecture, and promote the importance of sustainable design, and provides all manner of contracts for architecture and construction projects.

The AIA also works to educate the public about the benefits of good design and architecture, and advocates for policies and legislation that support the profession. The organization offers a range of services and programs for its members, including continuing education, professional development, networking opportunities, and access to resources such as research and publications.

In addition, the AIA is responsible for setting and enforcing ethical and professional standards for architects and provides accreditation for architecture programs at universities and other educational institutions. The organization is also involved in public outreach and education efforts such as the AIA Film Challenge, which invites filmmakers to create short films about the impact of architecture on communities. The AIA has national, state, and local chapters for areas across the United States.

AHJ (Authority Having Jurisdiction)

Authority Having Jurisdiction (AHJ) refers to an organization, agency, or individual that has the legal and administrative authority to enforce codes, ordinances, regulations, and standards within a particular jurisdiction.

AHJs are responsible for ensuring that buildings, construction projects, and other facilities are safe and comply with relevant codes and regulations. They also have the power to issue permits, conduct inspections, and approve plans for construction and other projects.

Baseboard

A baseboard is a long, narrow board that runs along the bottom of an interior wall, where the wall meets the floor. It is often made of wood and serves both a functional and decorative purpose. Functionally, baseboards protect the bottom of the wall from damage caused by foot traffic, furniture, and cleaning equipment. It also covers gaps between the flooring and the wall. Decoratively, baseboards can add an extra layer of design detail to a room, complementing the flooring and wall colors or patterns. Baseboards come in a variety of styles and heights, ranging from simple to ornate and intricate.

Blueprints

Blueprint is a legacy or historic term used for detailed technical drawings or 'plans' that are used in pricing, construction, engineering, and manufacturing to guide the building or production process. They are typically created by architects, engineers, or designers and include information such as dimensions, materials, and specifications. For the most part, the term 'plans' has replaced blueprints, as these drawings are no longer printed on specific blue paper. They are printed on bond paper instead.

Blueprints are an essential tool in the building process as they allow builders to have a detailed understanding of the project before construction begins. This can help to prevent costly mistakes and ensure that the final product meets the required specifications and standards.

Budget

A budget is a financial plan that is established after the project scope is adequately defined. It is designed by your architect and priced by your general contractor. It helps individuals and organizations to manage their money and make informed financial decisions. By creating and following a budget, individuals and organizations can track their financial progress, identify areas of overspending, and adjust plans to achieve their financial goals.

Cabinets

Cabinets are a type of case goods used for storage purposes. They typically consist of a box-shaped structure with doors, shelves, and sometimes drawers. Cabinets can be made from a variety of materials such as wood, metal, or plastic, and can be designed in a range of styles.

Cabinets are commonly used in kitchens to store cookware, utensils, and food items. They are also used in bathrooms to store toiletries and towels, and in bedrooms to store clothing and accessories. Cabinets can also be used in offices, garages, and other spaces for storage and organization purposes.

When selecting a cabinet, factors to consider include the size, materials, style, and functionality of the cabinet. It's important to choose a cabinet that can meet your storage needs while also fitting in with the overall look and feel of the room.

Case goods

Case goods is a term used in the furniture industry to refer to non-upholstered furniture such as cabinets, dressers, bookcases, desks, and other storage and display furniture made from wood or other materials. The term 'case goods' is derived from the fact that these types of furniture are typically constructed with a rigid framework or case, often made of wood or composite materials, that supports and protects the items stored within.

Case goods are typically made from a variety of materials such as solid wood, veneers, laminates, metal, and glass. The design and construction of case goods can vary widely depending on their intended use, style, and the materials used. For example, some case goods may have simple, traditional designs with minimal ornamentation, while others may have more elaborate, contemporary designs with intricate details and finishes.

Case goods are commonly used in residential, commercial, and hospitality settings, and can provide functional storage and display solutions while also adding aesthetic appeal to a space. When selecting case goods, factors such as durability, style, size, and functionality should be considered to ensure that the furniture meets the needs of the space and its users.

Change order

A construction change order is a document used in the construction industry to formally request or approve changes to the original scope of work or contract. Change orders are typically initiated when there is a change in the project scope, design, materials, or schedule, and may result in additional costs, time, or resources. The construction change order should include the following information:

- **Description of the change:** Clearly describe the proposed change, including drawings or specifications, if necessary.

- **Reason for the change:** Explain why the change is necessary and how it will impact the project.

- **Cost estimate:** Provide a detailed cost estimate for the change, including labor, materials, and any other expenses.

- **Schedule impact:** Describe how the change will affect the project schedule and any associated costs.

- **Approval signatures:** Include signatures from all relevant parties, such as the owner, contractor, and architect.

- **Effective date:** Specify the date the change order takes effect.

It is important to document any changes to the original contract in a change order to ensure that all parties agree and to avoid disputes or legal issues down the line.

Commissioning

Commissioning a building typically involves a series of processes to ensure that the building systems and components are designed, installed, and operate to meet the owner's requirements and expectations. After construction, the commissioning team works with the owner to train building operators and occupants, and to develop a plan for ongoing operations and maintenance.

Overall, commissioning a building is a collaborative effort between the owner, designers, contractors, and commissioning team to ensure that the building meets the owner's expectations and operates efficiently and reliably.

Cost (of construction)

The cost of construction can vary widely depending on several factors, including the location of the construction project, the type of building being constructed, the materials and labor required, and the complexity of the design.

In general, the cost of construction is typically calculated on a per-square-foot basis, which considers the total area of the building being constructed. Other factors that can affect the cost of construction include the cost of land, permits and fees, labor costs, materials costs, and any special requirements or features that need to be included in the building.

It is important to note that the cost of construction is not just limited to the actual construction of the building. Other costs that may need to be factored in include site preparation, excavation, demolition, and any necessary infrastructure improvements.

To get a more accurate estimate of the cost of construction for a specific project, it is best to consult with a construction professional or contractor who can provide a detailed breakdown of the costs involved.

Diagram

A diagram is a visual representation of information or data that is typically displayed in the form of a chart, graph, or other graphical format. Diagrams are used in a wide range of fields, including science, engineering, mathematics, and business to illustrate concepts, relationships, processes, and other types of information. They can be simple or complex and may be hand-drawn or created using computer software. Diagrams are often used to help communicate complex ideas or to provide a visual aid for understanding a concept or process.

Drawings (architectural)

Architectural drawings are visual representations of a building or structure that are created by architects, engineers, or drafters. These drawings provide detailed information about the design, dimensions, materials, and construction methods of a building. There are several types of architectural drawings, including:

- **Floor plans:** These show the layout of a building, including the position of walls, windows, doors, and other features.

- **Elevations:** These show the external appearance of a building, including its height, shape, and materials.

- **Sections:** These show a cutaway view of a building, revealing its internal structure and layout.

- **Details:** These show close-up views of specific features or construction methods such as windows, doors, or roofing.

Architectural drawings can be created using a variety of tools, including computer-aided design (CAD) software, hand-drawn sketches, or physical models. These drawings are an essential part of the construction process, providing a clear and detailed guide for builders and contractors to follow.

Elevations

Architectural elevations refer to the visual representation of a building's facade or exterior view. These elevations are usually depicted in two-dimensional drawings that show the building's height, width, and depth, as well as the placement of doors, windows, and other architectural features.

Architectural elevations are important because they provide a clear understanding of the overall design and style of a building. They help architects, builders, and clients visualize the final product and make important decisions about materials, colors, and finishes.

There are typically four types of elevations that are included in architectural drawings:

- **Front elevation:** This is the view of the building from the front, often referred to as the facade. It shows the entrance, the placement of windows, and other details on the building's front.

- **Rear elevation:** This is the view of the building from the rear, usually showing the placement of windows, doors, and other details on the back of the building.

- **Side elevation:** This is the view of the building from the side, showing the placement of windows, doors, and other details on either the left or right side of the building.

- **Cross-sectional elevation:** This is a view of the building cut through from top to bottom, showing details of the interior spaces, floors, and ceiling heights.

Overall, architectural elevations are an essential part of the design process for any building project. They help ensure that the final product meets the expectations of the client and complies with local building codes and regulations.

FFE (furniture, fixtures, and equipment)

Furniture, fixtures, and equipment are terms used in construction and design to describe the various items that are used to complete a building project:

- **Furniture** includes any movable object inside the building or home that is not attached to the walls, floors, or ceiling.

- **Fixtures** are permanent items that are attached to the building, such as light fixtures, sinks, toilets, and possibly built-in cabinets.

- **Equipment** refers to the items that are used in a building, such as furniture, appliances, and electronics, and in some cases mechanical, electrical, or plumbing equipment.

Together, furniture, fixtures, and equipment make up the final details that complete a building project. They play an important role in defining the overall look, feel, and functionality of a space.

Floor plan

A floor plan is a drawing that shows the layout of a building or a room, including the placement of walls, windows, doors, and furniture. Floor plans are typically used by architects, builders, and interior designers to help them understand the design of a project.

Floor plans can be created for various types of buildings, such as houses, apartments, offices, and commercial spaces. They may also include important details such as dimensions, room names, and locations of electrical outlets, plumbing fixtures, and other features.

Floor plans are an essential part of the design and construction process, as they help to ensure that a space is functional, efficient, and aesthetically pleasing.

General contractor

A general contractor is a professional who manages and oversees construction of projects from start to finish. They are responsible for coordinating and supervising all aspects of constructing a project, including hiring subcontractors, obtaining necessary permits, and ensuring that the project is completed on time and within budget.

General contractors typically work on construction projects such as commercial buildings, residential developments, infrastructure projects, and houses. They are responsible for ensuring that the project is completed according to the plans and specifications, and they are often the primary point of contact for the client or owner of the project.

HVAC (heating, ventilation, and air conditioning)

HVAC refers to the technology, systems, and equipment used to provide heating, cooling, and ventilation within buildings. HVAC systems are designed to regulate and maintain comfortable and healthy indoor air environments:

- **Heating** systems provide heating during cold weather to maintain a comfortable temperature. Common heating methods include furnaces, boilers, heat pumps, and electric heaters.

- **Ventilation** systems involve the exchange of indoor and outdoor air to improve air quality. They help remove pollutants, control humidity, and replenish oxygen. Ventilation can be achieved through natural means (such as open windows) or mechanical systems that use fans and ductwork.

- **Air conditioning** systems provide cooling during hot weather to lower indoor temperatures and control humidity levels. Air conditioners are used to cool the air and remove moisture. They can be centralized systems that cool the entire building or localized units for specific areas.

Components of HVAC systems include:

- **Thermostats:** Devices used to control and regulate temperature settings.

- **Furnaces or heat pumps:** Heating sources that generate warm air.

- **Air conditioners:** Cooling devices that remove heat from the air.

- **Ductwork:** Channels or pipes used to distribute conditioned air throughout the building.

- **Vents and registers:** Openings through which air enters or exits a room.
- **Fans:** Used to circulate air within the HVAC system and provide ventilation.
- **Filters:** Devices that capture dust, pollen, and other particles to improve air quality.
- **Humidifiers/dehumidifiers:** Equipment used to add or remove moisture from the air.
- **Exhaust systems:** Remove stale air, fumes, and odors from a building.

Proper installation, maintenance, and regular servicing of HVAC systems are important to ensure their efficient operation, energy savings, and a comfortable indoor environment.

Illustration

An illustration is a visual representation or depiction of a concept, idea, space, feature, object, etc. It can be created through various mediums such as painting, drawing, graphic design, or digital media. Illustrations are often used to enhance the understanding or communication of a message, story, or idea, and can be found in many different contexts. For architectural purposes, we use the term 'illustration' to mean drawings and renderings used to convey ideas about projects.

Lender

A lender is an individual, organization, or financial institution that loans money to a borrower with the expectation that the borrowed amount will be repaid with interest or other agreed-upon terms. Lenders can provide loans for a variety of purposes, including personal loans, business loans, mortgages, and auto loans. The terms and conditions of a loan agreement are typically negotiated between the lender and the borrower, and may include factors such as the interest rate, repayment period, and collateral requirements. Lenders may also assess a borrower's creditworthiness and ability to repay the loan before approving a loan application.

Lien waiver

A lien waiver is a legal document that waives or releases the right to place a lien on a property or assets. It is commonly used in construction and real estate transactions to protect property owners, lenders, and contractors.

When construction or improvement work is done on a property, contractors, subcontractors, and suppliers have the right to file a mechanic's lien if they are not paid for their services or materials. A mechanic's lien is a claim against the property, which can result in the property being sold to satisfy the debt.

To avoid potential disputes and ensure smooth transactions, parties involved in a construction project may request lien waivers from contractors, subcontractors, and suppliers. By signing a lien waiver, these parties agree to give up their right to file a lien against the property in exchange for payment for the rendered services.

There are different types of lien waivers, including:

- **Conditional lien waiver:** This type of waiver is used when a progress payment is made or promised, but has not yet been received. It waives the lien rights for the amount paid or promised.

- **Unconditional lien waiver:** This waiver is used when a payment has been received and clears the lien rights completely. It states that the payment has been received, and the right to file a lien is waived.

Lien waivers are typically exchanged between the parties involved in a construction project such as property owners, general contractors, subcontractors, and suppliers. They help protect the property owner from potential liens and ensure that contractors and suppliers receive timely payment for their work.

It's important to note that lien waiver requirements may vary by jurisdiction, so it's advisable to consult with a legal professional or familiarize yourself with the specific laws and regulations in your area before using or signing a lien waiver.

Millwork

Millwork refers to woodwork or any other wood-based building materials that have been produced in a mill or factory, usually for use in construction or home improvement projects. It can include items such as trim, moldings, doors, windows, and cabinetry. Millwork is typically manufactured to fit a specific project and can be customized to meet the individual needs and preferences of the customer. The term 'millwork' can also refer to the process of producing wood products in a mill or factory.

Millwork has become synonymous with case goods. (The meaning of case goods can be found above.)

OAC (Owner-Architect-Contractor) meetings

This is simply meetings between the owner, architect, and contractor. We have found that it is best for these to happen weekly or twice each month depending on the construction phase or specific schedule of the project. These meetings can be held on site or at the office of the contractor or architect. They are typically organized by the contractor and should have minutes recorded. This is the regular forum for questions to be asked and answered, as well as discussing current and upcoming schedules.

These meetings help to keep projects organized and ahead of any possible pitfalls. They are a crucial component to clear communication on your project during the construction or contract administration phase.

Pricing (construction)

Construction pricing can be a complex process that involves estimating the cost of materials, labor, equipment, and overhead expenses associated with a construction project. The pricing can vary depending on the location, size, and complexity of the project, as well as the availability and cost of materials and labor in the market.

Here are some factors that can affect construction pricing:

- **Type of project:** The type of construction project can impact pricing. For example, building a high-rise or a hospital may be more expensive than building a residential house.

- **Location:** Construction costs can vary by location due to differences in labor costs, material costs, and regulations. For example, construction costs in New York City may be higher than in a rural area.

- **Materials:** The cost of materials is a significant factor in construction pricing. The cost of materials can fluctuate depending on supply and demand, availability, and the distance the materials need to travel.

- **Labor:** The cost of labor is another significant factor in construction pricing. The cost of labor can vary depending on the location, experience level, and type of work being performed.

- **Equipment:** Certain construction projects may require specialized equipment such as cranes or bulldozers, which can add to the overall cost.

- **Overhead expenses:** Overhead expenses such as permits, insurance, and administrative costs can also affect the final construction pricing.

To determine construction pricing, contractors typically use a process called 'estimating'. They evaluate the cost of materials, labor, and other factors to create a detailed estimate of the total project cost. This estimate is typically provided to the client as a proposal or bid, which outlines the project scope, timeline, and total cost.

Once pricing has been estimated, a budget for the project can be established by adding all the ancillary soft and other costs to create a holistic financial picture for the project.

Prime consultant

A prime consultant, also known as a lead consultant or a main consultant, is a professional or consulting firm that is responsible for overseeing and coordinating a project from conception to completion. In the context of construction and engineering projects, the prime consultant is typically an architecture or engineering firm.

The role of a prime consultant may vary depending on the specific project and industry, but generally, their responsibilities include:

- **Project coordination:** The prime consultant acts as the main point of contact and coordinator for the project. They collaborate with various stakeholders, including clients, subconsultants, contractors, and regulatory authorities.

- **Design management:** The prime consultant often takes the lead in the design phase of a project. They develop the initial concept, prepare design briefs, coordinate with other design disciplines, and ensure that the design aligns with the client's requirements and project objectives.

- **Technical expertise:** Prime consultants typically possess specialized technical knowledge in their respective fields. They provide expertise and guidance throughout the project, ensuring that design and construction activities meet applicable codes, standards, and regulations.

- **Contract administration:** The prime consultant may assist the client in preparing contract documents, evaluating bids or proposals, and managing contracts with subconsultants and contractors. They help in reviewing and approving payments, change orders, and other contractual matters.

- **Project management:** Prime consultants often assume project management responsibilities, including scheduling, cost control, quality assurance, and risk management. They monitor project progress, identify and mitigate potential issues, and ensure timely delivery within the allocated budget.

- **Stakeholder communication:** Effective communication is crucial in project management. Prime consultants facilitate communication among project team members, stakeholders, and authorities having jurisdiction. They provide regular updates, address concerns, and maintain positive working relationships.

It's important to note that the exact scope of a prime consultant's role can vary depending on the project and contractual arrangements. In some cases, the prime consultant may take on additional responsibilities such as obtaining permits and approvals, conducting feasibility studies, or providing post-construction services.

Reimbursable expense

A reimbursable expense refers to an expense that an individual or entity pays for on behalf of another person or organization, with the understanding that they will be reimbursed for the amount spent. Reimbursable expenses typically occur in situations where one party incurs costs on behalf of another party for a specific purpose such as business travel, supplies, or services.

Rendering

Rendering refers to the process of generating an image, animation, or video from a three-dimensional model. Architects use 3D models of their projects to generate renderings to communicate the project design and intent to the client and other stakeholders.

Overall, rendering is an essential part of the visual media creation process, allowing designers and artists to bring their ideas to life in a way that is both realistic and engaging.

Reveal (architectural)

An architectural reveal is a design feature in architecture where a portion of a building or structure is intentionally left exposed or visible to showcase its construction, materials, or design details. Reveals can be created by cutting away or recessing parts of the building's exterior or interior surfaces such as walls or ceilings to create shadow lines or depth.

Reveals are often used to highlight the beauty of raw materials like concrete, brick, or wood, or to accentuate the symmetry or geometric shapes of a building's design. Additionally, they can serve a functional purpose such as providing ventilation or concealing electrical wiring or plumbing.

Architectural reveals can add interest and character to a building and are commonly used in modern and contemporary architecture. They can be found in various forms, including window reveals, door reveals, and corner reveals.

Schedule (architectural)

An architectural schedule is a document that outlines the timeline and milestones for a construction project. The schedule typically includes information about when various stages of the project will be completed, when specific tasks will be undertaken, and when resources will be allocated.

It's essential to have an accurate architectural schedule that is updated regularly to ensure that the project is progressing as planned and to identify any potential delays or issues that need to be addressed.

Scope

Architectural scope refers to the overall range or extent of a particular architectural project or initiative. It encompasses the objectives, requirements, and constraints that shape the design and implementation of a building or structure. In general, the architectural scope includes the following aspects:

- **Purpose:** The intended use of the building or structure and the needs it must fulfill.

- **Site and context:** The location of the building or structure and the physical, social, and cultural factors that affect its design.

- **Space planning and programming:** The arrangement of spaces and functions within the building or structure to support its intended use.

- **Building systems and technology:** The selection and integration of building systems and technology to support the building's operation and maintenance.

- **Sustainability and environmental impact:** The design and construction of the building or structure to minimize its environmental impact and promote sustainability.

- **Aesthetics and style:** The visual and aesthetic qualities of the building or structure, including its form, materials, and detailing.

The architectural scope may vary depending on the specific project and its context. It is essential to define it clearly at the outset of the project to guide the design process and ensure that the outcome meets the stakeholders' needs and expectations.

Scope creep

Scope creep refers to the gradual and unauthorized expansion of a project's goals, requirements, and deliverables beyond the original scope. It can occur due to a variety of reasons such as poor project planning, lack of stakeholder involvement, inadequate requirements gathering, or changing business needs.

Scope creep can have significant consequences for a project such as increased costs, delayed timelines, and reduced quality. It can also lead to conflicts between project stakeholders, as the project team may feel that they are being asked to do more work without sufficient resources or time.

To prevent scope creep, it's essential to have a well-defined project scope that is agreed upon by all stakeholders. The project scope should clearly outline the project's goals, deliverables, timelines, and budget. Any changes to the scope should be approved by the project sponsor and communicated to all stakeholders.

Effective communication and stakeholder management are also critical to prevent scope creep. Regular meetings, progress reports, and feedback sessions can help ensure that everyone is aligned on the project's goals and expectations. Additionally, using project management tools and techniques such as a work breakdown structure can help identify potential scope creep and mitigate its impact on the project.

Section (architectural)

An architectural section refers to a vertical cut or slice through a building or structure that reveals its interior spaces, structural system, and other details. It is a two-dimensional representation of a three-dimensional space that helps architects, engineers, and builders understand the relationships between different building elements and how they function together.

Architectural sections are typically created using computer-aided design (CAD) software, which allows designers to create accurate and detailed representations of building sections. They may include information on the thickness of walls, the height of ceilings, the placement of doors and windows, the location of electrical and plumbing systems, and other details that are critical to the construction process.

Architectural sections are an essential part of the design and construction process, as they help to ensure that buildings are structurally sound, meet building codes and regulations, and are aesthetically pleasing. They are also used by contractors and builders to estimate construction costs and plan construction sequencing.

Subcontractor

A subcontractor is a person or company that is hired by a contractor to perform a specific task or project as part of a larger contract or project. The subcontractor typically has expertise in a specific area or trade such as an electrician, tile installer, drywaller, etc, and is brought on to complete a specific portion of the work. The subcontractor is not typically an employee of the contractor, but rather an independent contractor or vendor. The subcontractor is responsible for providing their own tools, equipment, and materials, and is typically paid by the contractor for the completion of the agreed-upon work.

Trim (architectural)

Architectural trim is designed to cover transitions between materials, for example, drywall and wood door/window frames. Also known as molding or millwork, trim refers to the decorative elements that are used to enhance the appearance of a building or room. These decorative elements include baseboards, crown molding, door and window casings, wainscoting, and chair rails:

- **Baseboards** are installed along the bottom of walls, where they meet the floor. They help to cover the gap between the wall and the floor.

- **Crown molding** is installed where the ceiling meets the wall, providing a decorative transition between the two surfaces. It can be simple or elaborate, depending on the style of the room.

- **Door and window casings** are the frames around doors and windows. They provide a decorative element to the room and they cover gaps between the wall and the door or window frame.

- **Wainscoting** is a type of paneling that covers the lower portion of a wall, usually up to chair rail height. It can be made of wood or other materials and can add a decorative touch to a room.

- **Chair rails** are installed at the top of wainscoting or at a height of about 3ft from the floor. They provide a visual break between the lower and upper portions of the wall and can also protect the wall from damage caused by chairs and other furniture.

Overall, architectural trim can enhance the look and feel of a building or room, adding both beauty and function. (The opposite of trim is 'reveal', the meaning of which can be found above.)

Work product

Work product refers to the output or results of one's work. For an architecture or design project, work product refers to the drawings, diagrams, specifications, research, renderings, illustrations, etc, that are produced during the course of creating and communicating a project to the client and other various stakeholders.

Directory

For the AIA and Canadian Associations below, the areas of interest should be the Awards pages, where it is possible to see the submissions and winners from each year. This would give an indication of which firms in your area are participating in these programs and who is winning. These have galleries for the submission with portfolio pictures for viewing the projects.

The firm/practice listings may only give links to contact information, which might prove to be a laborious task to then find firms that align with the type of project you are trying to accomplish.

SPEAKING ARCHITECTURE

American Institute of Architects major city chapters

AIA National – www.aia.org

Chicago – https://aiachicago.org
(find an architect tab)

New York – www.aiany.org
(resources/ firm directory)

Los Angeles – www.aialosangeles.org

Houston – https://aiahouston.org
(resources/find a firm)

Phoenix – http://aia-phoenixmetro.org

Philadelphia – https://aiaphiladelphia.org
(find an architect)

San Antonio – https://aiasa.org
(resources/find an architect)

San Diego – https://aiasandiego.org
(directory/ architect finder)

Dallas – www.aiadallas.org
(expertise/folio-find a firm)

San Jose – https://aiasiliconvalley.org
(architect directory)

DIRECTORY

Canadian architectural associations

British Columbia – https://aibc.ca (find an architect)

Alberta – www.aaa.ab.ca
(public resource/ member directory)

Saskatchewan – https://saskarchitects.com
(public resource/member directory)

Manitoba – www.mbarchitects.org
(about/members and firms)

Ontario – https://oaa.on.ca (OAA directory)

Quebec – www.oaq.com

New Brunswick – www.aanb.org (find an architect)

PEI – https://aapei.com (find an architect)

Nova Scotia – https://nsaa.ns.ca
(hire an architect/ search our members)

Newfoundland – https://newfoundlandarchitects.com/Home (find an architect)

Yukon – https://yukon.ca/en/department-highways-public-works

NWT – www.nwtaa.ca (public/member directory)

Nunavut – www.gov.nu.ca/community-and-government-services

201

Educational

Below are links to schools of architecture for reference. It may be worth having a look at schools of architecture to understand what is happening in your city. Also of note could be the faculty pages. Many architects that teach also maintain practices and have great knowledge about the city in which they are located. These institutions have yearly public shows and lecture series. The year-end shows are very inspirational and a nice way to see great work and connect with your community.

Chicago

IIT College of Architecture – https://arch.iit.edu

UIC School of Architecture – https://arch.uic.edu

SAIC AIADO – www.saic.edu/aiado

Top US graduate schools of architecture

Harvard – www.gsd.harvard.edu/architecture

Columbia – www.arch.columbia.edu

MIT – https://architecture.mit.edu

Yale – www.architecture.yale.edu

Cornell – https://aap.cornell.edu/academics/architecture/graduate

Princeton – https://soa.princeton.edu

Rice – https://arch.rice.edu

Rhode Island School of Design – www.risd.edu/academics/architecture

Penn – www.design.upenn.edu/master-architecture-professional-degree

Berkeley – https://ced.berkeley.edu/arch/degrees-admissions/master-of-architecture

Top US undergrad schools of architecture

Virginia Polytechnic – https://aad.vt.edu

Cornell – https://aap.cornell.edu/academics/architecture

Syracuse – https://soa.syr.edu

California Polytechnic – https://architecture.calpoly.edu

University of Texas at Austin – https://soa.utexas.edu

Carnegie Mellon – https://soa.cmu.edu

Kansas State – https://apdesign.k-state.edu

Pennsylvania State – https://arts.psu.edu/academics/department-of-architecture

Pratt Institute – www.pratt.edu/architecture

Cultural

North America has world-class architecture and design institutions. Consider visiting the ones in your own community or while on your next trip.

AIA New York – Center for Architecture – www.centerforarchitecture.org

Architecture + Design Museum – https://aplusd.org

Art, Design & Architecture Museum – www.museum.ucsb.edu

Chicago Architecture Center – www.architecture.org

Chicago Athenaeum – www.chi-athenaeum.org

Edith Farnsworth House – https://edithfarnsworthhouse.org

Glass House – https://theglasshouse.org

Graham Foundation – www.grahamfoundation.org

Museum of Design Atlanta – www.museumofdesign.org

National Building Museum – www.nbm.org

National Building Arts Center – http://web.nationalbuildingarts.org

Skyscraper Museum – https://skyscraper.org

Storefront for Art & Architecture – https://storefrontnews.org

DIRECTORY

Aga Kahn Museum – https://agakhanmuseum.org

Canadian Center for Architecture – www.cca.qc.ca/en

Canadian Museum of Architecture – https://cmarch.ca

Royal Ontario Museum – www.rom.on.ca

Print online magazines

There are many resources available as physical publications and digital magazines. These may be preferred to social media for assembling client precedent packages to communicate to your architect and design team.

Architectural Digest – www.architecturaldigest.com

Arch Daily – www.archdaily.com

Architect – www.architectmagazine.com

Architect's Newspaper – www.archpaper.com

Architectural Record – www.architecturalrecord.com

The Architectural Review – www.architectural-review.com

Architizer – https://architizer.com

Azure – www.azuremagazine.com

Canadian Architect – www.canadianarchitect.com

Design Boom – www.designboom.com

Detail – www.detail.de/de_en

Dezeen – www.dezeen.com

Domus – www.domusweb.it/en.html

Dwell – www.dwell.com

El Croquis – https://elcroquis.es

Frame – www.frameweb.com

Interior Design – https://interiordesign.net

Metropolis – https://metropolismag.com

Surface Magazine – www.surfacemag.com

Wallpaper – www.wallpaper.com

Acknowledgments

I wrote this book because I believe architects to be prolific at communicating with each other and our industry; this is inward communication. However, there could be a much more successful effort helping clients and the general public understand what architects do and how they work. What is an architecture project? What does the basic architecture process look like? This book became the opportunity to explain this architectural process from our perspective, to create a resource for clients that can be used on their own time, away from the meeting room and jobsite, without stress or pressure.

I would like to express my gratitude to Trevor Lord, Rick Nelson, Carlo Parente, and Lamar Johnson for taking the time to work through the draft copy of the book in order to bring this project to life. Your feedback was instrumental in bringing this book to life. And many thanks to Collective Office, Tyler Moench, Preston Smith, and Clayton Pangrcic for the steadfast work, collaboration, and dedication to the practice of architecture and our office.

I would also like to thank Donny Mangos for, well, bringing the energy that started this entire project. I thank you for being the friend of friends!

The Author

Jeff Klymson is an architect, educator, and author. He is the founding principal of Collective Office – an architecture and design practice working on modern residential, workplace, and retail projects in North America. He taught architecture as an adjunct professor at Illinois Institute of Technology ('07–'17). During this time, Jeff delivered lectures, instruction, and guidance to more than 300 students at IIT, and as a guest critic at University of Illinois at Chicago and the School of the Art Institute. Jeff is a passionate lifelong learner in the discipline of architecture and design.

Jeff is a husband and father residing in Chicago, Illinois. He was born and raised in Vancouver, BC and then transitioned with his family and was educated in Toronto and then Chicago. Jeff studied architecture at Toronto Metropolitan University (B.Arch '00) and then at Illinois Institute of Technology (M.Arch '06). He is a professionally licensed architect in fifteen states, and Ontario Canada. Jeff created the practice Collective Office in 2009 to focus on the practice and research of design through the lens of architecture. Collective Office provides a project-specific, detail-oriented process for research and projects. Jeff employs this process on all projects to challenge conventions, push boundaries, and ask questions at every stage of the process. The principal focus of his research is the convergence of architecture and the branded world to create personal experiences. His continual aim is to use this idea to create a more intuitive connection for people within their own built environments.

Collective Office can be found at

🌐 www.collectiveoffice.com

📷 @collective_office / 312-818-2006.

www.ingramcontent.com/pod-product-compliance
Lightning Source LLC
Chambersburg PA
CBHW050525170426
43201CB00013B/2083